Appliqué Jubilee

16 QUILT PROJECTS WITH HAND, MACHINE & FUSIBLE APPLIQUÉ

*From the Editors and Contributors
of McCall's Quilting*

C&T PUBLISHING

Text and artwork copyright © 2008 by CK Media

Publisher: *Amy Marson*

Creative Director: *Gailen Runge*

Acquisitions Editor: *Jan Grigsby*

Editors: *Kesel Wilson, Lynn Koolish,* and *Cynthia Bix*

Technical Editor: *Joyce Lytle*

Proofreader: *Wordfirm, Inc.*

Cover Designer: *Kristy Zacharias*

Book Designer: *Rose Sheifer-Wright*

Production Coordinator: *Kirstie L. Pettersen*

Published by C&T Publishing, Inc., P.O. Box 1456, Lafayette, CA 94549

Library of Congress Cataloging-in-Publication Data
Appliqué jubilee : 16 quilt projects with hand, machine & fusible appliqué / from the editors and contributors of McCall's quilting.
    p. cm.
  Summary: "A compilation of 16 projects from McCall's Quilting magazine featuring patchwork with appliqué. Projects include full-sized templates"— Provided by publisher.
  ISBN 978-1-57120-574-2 (paper trade : alk. paper)
 1. Appliqué--Patterns. 2. Patchwork--Patterns. I. McCall's quilting.

TT779.A64 2008
746.44'5041--dc22

Printed in China

10 9 8 7 6 5 4 3 2 1

CONTENTS

INTRODUCTION

While I love quilting in all its forms, I have to admit that nothing lifts my spirits in quite the same way as a beautiful appliqué quilt. The soft curves that appliqué elements can bring to an otherwise geometric pieced quilt; the elegance of winding stems and leaves; the cheery feeling that radiates from a bouquet of appliqué flowers—I cherish them all.

That's why I'm so pleased to present this book that celebrates appliqué in all its joyous variety. The 16 projects in the book were chosen from issues of *McCall's Quilting* spanning a three-year period. Whatever color palette or style of appliqué you like best, I'm sure you will find something here that cries, "Make me!" If the instructions for the quilt you choose to make are for a different appliqué technique than the one you prefer, it's easy to adapt the template patterns to your favorite technique.

In addition to the detailed cutting charts and instructions for the individual projects, you can also refer to the chapter on quiltmaking basics for help with constructing, quilting, or finishing your projects.

Whether you make these quilts for yourself or as gifts to be treasured for a lifetime, I wish you the same joy in creating them that we had in collecting them for you. Happy appliquéing!

Beth Hayes
Editor-in-Chief
McCall's Quilting

Ferns & Florals

Photographed at Echter's Greenhouse and Gardens,
5150 Garrison Street, Arvada, CO 80002

Skill Level 3

Designed by Vicki Hoskins.

Machine quilted by Phyllis Reddish.

Finished quilt size: 48″ × 68″

Number of blocks & finished size:
8 pieced blocks 10″ × 10″
7 appliquéd blocks 10″ × 10″

Marry beautiful pieced and appliquéd blocks with tranquil colors and the results are the pure and absolute bliss you find every time you look at this quilt.

Fabric Requirements and Cutting Instructions

PLANNING

The beige large floral squares are cut $7\frac{9}{16}$″. If you are not familiar with cutting $\frac{1}{16}$″ intervals, note that $\frac{9}{16}$″ is halfway between $\frac{1}{2}$″ and $\frac{5}{8}$″.

To fussy-cut the $7\frac{9}{16}$″ squares from the beige large floral print, make a template from clear template plastic. Include seamlines so you can center the motif. Place the template on the floral motif, centering as desired. Mark around the edge of the template and cut it out.

FABRIC	AMOUNT	CUTTING
		See the Pullout at the back of the book for template pattern. Appliqué template is printed without seam allowances.
Cream texture (background)	$1\frac{1}{2}$ yards	*7 squares 12″ × 12″ 64 squares $1\frac{3}{4}$″ × $1\frac{3}{4}$″ 64 squares $2\frac{1}{8}$″ × $2\frac{1}{8}$″, cut in half diagonally to make 128 half-square triangles
Green texture (piecing)	$\frac{1}{4}$ yard	48 squares $1\frac{3}{4}$″ × $1\frac{3}{4}$″
Red texture (piecing, middle border)	$\frac{1}{2}$ yard	*2 strips $1\frac{3}{4}$″ × 56″, pieced from 3 width of fabric (WOF) strips *2 strips $1\frac{3}{4}$″ × WOF 48 squares $1\frac{3}{4}$″ × $1\frac{3}{4}$″
Blue texture (piecing)	$\frac{1}{4}$ yard	32 squares $1\frac{3}{4}$″ × $1\frac{3}{4}$″
Beige large floral (piecing)	**$1\frac{1}{4}$ yards	***8 squares $7\frac{9}{16}$″ × $7\frac{9}{16}$″
Green tone-on-tone (stems, leaves)	$\frac{3}{4}$ yard	14 strips 1″ × $10\frac{1}{2}$″ 168 Template A
Light blue texture (buds)	$\frac{3}{8}$ yard	84 Template A
Light brown texture (inner border)	$\frac{1}{2}$ yard	2 strips 2″ × 53″, pieced from 3 WOF strips 2 strips 2″ × WOF
Blue small floral (outer border, binding)	$1\frac{7}{8}$ yards	2 strips $6\frac{1}{2}$″ × 59″, cut on the lengthwise grain 2 strips $6\frac{1}{2}$″ × 51″, cut on the lengthwise grain
Backing (piece horizontally)	$3\frac{1}{4}$ yards	
Batting	Twin size	
OTHER MATERIALS		
Template plastic (optional for fussy-cutting)		
$\frac{1}{4}$″ bias bar (optional)		

**Cut first.* ***Yardage based on featured fabric.* ****See Planning.*

Piecing and Appliquéing the Blocks

See Basic Quiltmaking Instructions, pages 65–70, for instructions on appliqué.

1. Arrange and sew rows using cream texture and green texture $1\frac{3}{4}''$ squares and cream texture $2\frac{1}{8}''$ half-square triangles. Sew the rows together to make pieced triangles. Press. Make 12. Repeat this process, using red texture squares and blue texture squares; make quantities as shown.

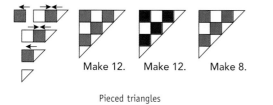

Make 12.   Make 12.   Make 8.

Pieced triangles

2. Sew matching pieced triangles to the sides of a beige large floral $7\frac{9}{16}''$ square to make a pieced block. Press seams toward the floral square. Make 8 total.

Make 3 green, 3 red, 2 blue.

Pieced block

3. Fold $1'' \times 10\frac{1}{2}''$ green tone-on-tone strips in half, wrong sides together. Stitch $\frac{1}{4}''$ from the raw edge. Trim the seam allowance to $\frac{1}{8}''$. Press the tube flat, centering the seam allowance on the back so the raw edge isn't visible from the front. Using a $\frac{1}{4}''$ bias bar makes pressing faster and easier. Make 14.

Make 14.

Stem tube

4. **Note:** The cream texture appliqué background squares are cut over-sized to allow for shrinkage during appliqué. Finger-press a cream texture $12''$ square in half diagonally twice; use the folds as a placement guide. Position green tone-on-tone stems and template fabrics, keeping in mind that the square will be trimmed to $10\frac{1}{2}'' \times 10\frac{1}{2}''$ (finished size is $10''$ square). Using the appliqué method of your choice, appliqué in place. Trim to $10\frac{1}{2}''$ square. Make 7 appliqué blocks.

Make 7.

Positioning the appliqué

Quilt Top Assembly

Refer to the assembly diagram for the following steps.

1. Arrange and sew 5 rows alternating pieced blocks with appliquéd blocks. Sew the rows together. Press seams open. Sew light brown texture $2'' \times 53''$ strips to the sides; trim even with the top and bottom. Stitch the remaining light brown texture strips to the top/bottom; trim even with the sides.

2. Stitch red texture $1\frac{3}{4}'' \times 56''$ strips to the sides; trim even. Sew the remaining red texture strips to the top/bottom; trim even. Sew blue small floral $6\frac{1}{2}'' \times 59''$ strips to the sides; trim even. Stitch the remaining blue small floral strips to the top/bottom; trim even.

Assembly diagram

Quilting and Finishing

See Basic Quiltmaking Instructions, pages 65–70, for instructions on quilting and binding.

1. Layer and baste the quilt top for the quilting method of your choice. Phyllis machine ditch quilted the appliqué and blocks. The corners of the pieced blocks are crosshatched, and a floral motif is centered on the fussy-cut squares. Flowing floral leaf vines fill the borders.

2. Bind the quilt with blue small floral fabric.

Lavender & Thyme

Skill Level 3

Designed by Julie Sheckman.

Finished quilt size: $53^1/2'' \times 53^1/2''$

Number of blocks & finished size:
4 Lavender & Thyme blocks 20″ × 20″

Savor the beauty as you piece and appliqué this lovely wallhanging. Julie's unique appliqué method uses Mettler Cordonnet topstitching thread to finish the edges of the motifs and to add texture and movement throughout the quilt.

Fabric Requirements and Cutting Instructions

Julie made this dramatic quilt by piecing the background and appliquéing the leaves, circles, and half-circles, using paper-backed fusible web.

FABRIC	AMOUNT	CUTTING
		See the Pullout at the back of the book for template patterns. Appliqué template patterns are printed without seam allowances. Piecing template patterns are printed with seam allowances.
Tan/rust floral and navy vine print (block)	$^7/8$ yard each	32 Template A from each
Cream vine print and cream mottle (block)	$^5/8$ yard each	32 Template B from each
Navy print and rust print (block)	$^1/4$ yard each	32 Template C from each
Purple print (oak leaves)	$^3/4$ yard	48 Template D
		8 Template G
Green print (small leaves)	$^1/4$ yard	48 Template E
Tan print (circles, half circles)	$^1/8$ yard	16 Template F
		12 Template H
Blue stripe (inner border)	$^3/8$ yard	2 strips $1^1/2'' \times$ width of fabric (WOF)
		2 strips $1^1/2'' \times 46''$, pieced from 3 WOF strips
Navy large floral (outer border)	$1^3/4$ yards	2 strips 6″ × 47″, cut on lengthwise grain
		2 strips 6″ × 57″, cut on lengthwise grain
Dark gold stripe (bias-cut binding)	$^7/8$ yard	
Backing	$3^1/2$ yards	
Batting	Twin size	
OTHER MATERIALS		
Paper-backed fusible web	$2^1/4$ yards	
Mettler Cordonnet thread: navy, rust		
Monofilament thread		
Gold/cream variegated thread		
Size 90/14 or 100/16 sewing machine needle		
Seam sealant (optional)		

Piecing the Blocks

1. Stitch Template A tan/rust floral, Template B cream vine print, and Template C navy print together to make a pieced square. Be sure to align the dots. Clip, pin, or baste the curved seams. Repeat this process using Template A navy vine print, Template B cream mottle, and Template C rust print. Make 32 of each. Press.

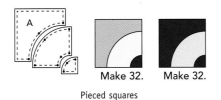

Make 32. Make 32.

Pieced squares

2. Arrange and sew 4 rows using pieced squares in the color arrangement as shown. Sew the rows together to make Lavender & Thyme blocks. Make 2 of each block arrangement.

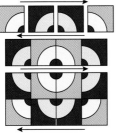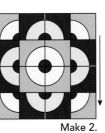

Make 2.

Lavender & Thyme block 1

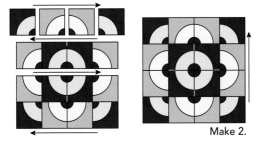

Make 2.

Lavender & Thyme block 2

Quilt Top Assembly

Refer to Assembly diagram 1 for the following steps.

1. Arrange and sew 2 rows of 2 blocks each. Press. Sew the rows together. Press. Sew blue stripe 1½″ × WOF strips to the sides; trim even with the top and bottom. Stitch the remaining blue stripe strips to the top/bottom; trim even with the sides.

2. Sew navy large floral 6″ × 47″ strips to the sides; trim even with the top/bottom. Stitch the remaining navy large floral strips to the top/bottom; trim even with the sides.

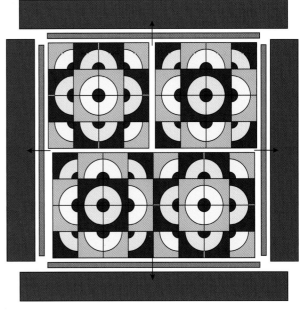

Assembly diagram 1

Adding the Appliqué

See Basic Quiltmaking Instructions, pages 65–70, for instructions on appliqué.

1. Trace Templates D–H on the paper side of paper-backed fusible web. Cut apart, leaving a small margin beyond the drawn lines. Following the manufacturer's instructions, fuse to the wrong side of the appropriate fabrics; cut apart on the drawn line.

2. Referring to Assembly diagram 2, page 10, position Templates D–H. Following the manufacturer's instructions, fuse in place. **Note:** If you're concerned that the appliqué edges may fray, apply seam sealant to them, but test a small area first for colorfastness.

3. Add decorative stitching around the appliqués in the following manner. Insert a size 90/14 or 100/16 needle into the machine and set the stitch length at approximately 9 stitches per inch. Using rust (for Lavender & Thyme blocks 1) and navy (for Lavender & Thyme blocks 2) Mettler Cordonnet thread in the needle and all-purpose thread in the bobbin, Julie stitched next to the template edge, leaving enough thread at the beginning and end to pull to the back and tie off. For best results, stitch slowly and use an appliqué or open-toe foot.

Quilting and Finishing

See Basic Quiltmaking Instructions, pages 65–70, for instructions on quilting and binding.

1. Layer and baste the quilt top for the quilting method of your choice. Julie machine ditch quilted the appliqué and seamlines using monofilament thread. She added a meander in the borders. Using a gold/cream variegated thread, she added a wavy vein in the center of each oak leaf.

2. Bind the quilt with bias-cut dark gold stripe fabric.

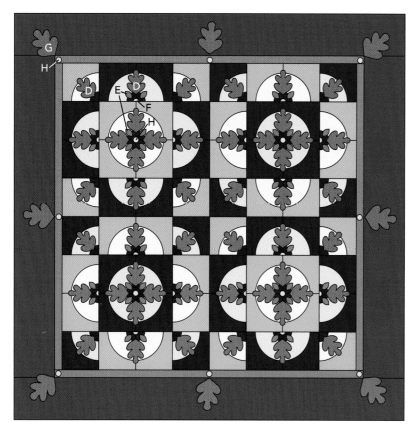

Assembly diagram 2

Daisy Chain

Designed by Nancy Mahoney.

Finished quilt size: 55″ × 55″

Number of blocks & finished size:

16 Stepping Stone blocks 8″ × 8″

9 appliquéd Daisy blocks 8″ × 8″

　　Toast spring with a flurry of freshly stitched daises. Have fun creating these cheery appliquéd flowers that you can enjoy all year long, no matter what the weather.

Fabric Requirements and Cutting Instructions

Using strip sets to make the Stepping Stone blocks will speed construction along so you will have plenty of time to perfect your appliqué stitch on the Daisy blocks!

FABRIC	AMOUNT	CUTTING
		See the Pullout at the back of the book for template patterns. Appliqué template patterns are printed without seam allowances.
Blue print (blocks, border, binding)	3 yards	*4 strips 5″ × 59″, cut on lengthwise grain
		*8 strips 2″ × width of fabric (WOF)
		*1 strip 2½″ × WOF
		9 each Templates B–G
Cream print (background, setting triangles)	2¼ yards	*2 strips 2½″ × WOF
		*2 strips 2″ × WOF
		*2 strips 5½″ × WOF
		*3 squares 13¼″ × 13¼″, cut in half twice diagonally to make 12 quarter-square triangles
		*9 squares 9″ × 9″
		*2 squares 7″ × 7″, cut in half diagonally to make 4 half-square triangles
		32 strips 2″ × 5½″
Green print (stems, leaves)	⅜ yard	*9 strips 1″ × 5″ (bias cut)
		9 each Templates A/Ar
Yellow print (flower center)	6″ × 6″ piece	9 Template H
Backing	3⅝ yards	
Batting	Twin size	
OTHER MATERIALS		
Bias bar, ¼″ (optional)		

Cut first.

Piecing and Appliquéing the Blocks

See Basic Quiltmaking Instructions, pages 65–70, for instructions on appliqué.

1. Sew blue print and cream print strips together in sizes shown and quantities of strip sets indicated below. Press seams in direction of the arrows. Cut segments the sizes indicated in quantities shown for each strip set.

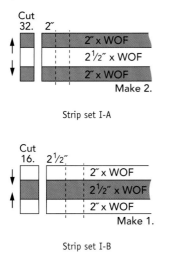

Strip set I-A

Strip set I-B

Strip set I-C

2. Sew I-A and I-B strip segments together to make a pieced square. Press seams open.

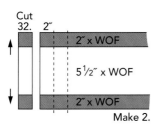

Pieced square

3. Sew cream print 2″ × 5½″ strips to the sides of the pieced square and I-C strip segments to the top and bottom to make Stepping Stone blocks. Make 16.

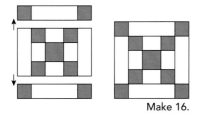

Stepping Stone block

4. To make stems, fold green print 1″ × 5″ bias-cut strips in half, wrong sides together. Stitch ¼″ from the raw edge. Trim the seam allowance to ⅛″. Press the tube flat, centering the seam allowance on the back so the raw edge isn't visible from the front. Using a ¼″ bias bar makes pressing faster and easier. Trim the stem to 4¾″. Make 9.

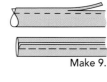

Make 9.

Stem bias tube

5. **Note:** The cream print appliqué background squares are cut oversized to allow for shrinkage during appliqué. Finger-press a cream print 9″ square in half diagonally twice; use the folds as a placement guide. Position the stem and Template fabrics A–H, keeping in mind that the square will be trimmed to 8½″ × 8½″ (finished size is 8″ × 8″). Using the appliqué method of your choice, appliqué in place. Trim to 8½″ square, centering the appliqué. Make 9. **Note:** Nancy machine buttonhole stitched around her appliqué with matching thread. Do likewise if you wish.

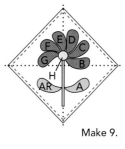

Make 9.

Positioning the appliqué

Quilt Top Assembly

Refer to the assembly diagram, page 14, for the following steps.

Note: The setting triangles on all edges and corners are cut oversized to allow trimming the quilt edges even after assembly.

1. Arrange and stitch 7 diagonal rows using cream print 13¼″ quarter-square triangles and blocks. Sew the rows together. Stitch cream print 7″ half-square triangles to the corners. Trim the quilt edges even.

2. Sew blue print 5″ × 59″ strips to the sides; trim even with the top and bottom. Stitch the remaining blue print strips to the top/bottom; trim even with the sides.

Quilting and Finishing

See Basic Quiltmaking Instructions, pages 65–70, for instructions on quilting and binding.

1. Layer and baste the quilt top for the quilting method of your choice. Nancy machine ditch quilted the seams and appliqué. She added a motif on the setting triangles and a meander on the border.

2. Bind the quilt with blue print fabric.

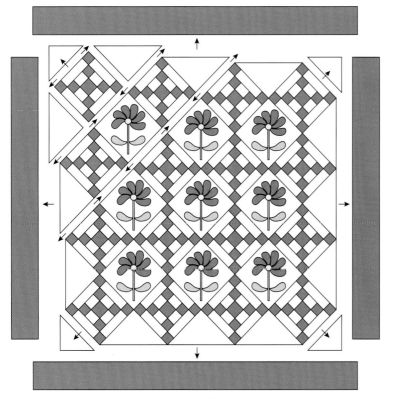

Assembly diagram

Lazy Daisy Baskets

Skill Level 3

Designed by Ann Weber.

Finished quilt size: 48″ × 48″

Number of blocks & finished size:
4 Basket blocks 12″ × 12″

The old-fashioned beauty of daisies never goes out of style and neither will this charming quilt. Piece your basket blocks, and then pick a favorite gold print to appliqué the delightful trail of blooming beauties.

Fabric Requirements and Cutting Instructions

FABRIC	AMOUNT	CUTTING
		See the Pullout at the back of the book for template patterns. Appliqué template patterns are printed without seam allowances. Piecing template patterns are printed with seam allowances.
Medium blue mottle (baskets, outer border)	1¼ yards	*4 strips 6¼″ × 40″ 4 strips 1½″ × 8½″ 4 strips 1½″ × 9½″ 2 squares 5⅞″ × 5⅞″, cut in half diagonally to make 4 half-square triangles 4 squares 2⅞″ × 2⅞″, cut in half diagonally to make 8 half-square triangles
Cream print (block background)	⅝ yard	2 squares 6⅞″ × 6⅞″, cut in half diagonally to make 4 half-square triangles 8 strips 2½″ × 6½″ 4 strips 2½″ × 10½″ 4 strips 2½″ × 12½″ 2 squares 4⅞″ × 4⅞″, cut in half diagonally to make 4 half-square triangles
Blue/cream stripe (baskets)	¼ yard	4 Template A
Light blue print (background)	1 yard	*1 square 19″ × 19″, cut in half twice diagonally to make 4 quarter-square triangles 1 square 12½″ × 12½″ 2 squares 10″ × 10″, cut in half diagonally to make 4 half-square triangles
Light brown print (inner border, binding)	⅞ yard	4 strips 1½″ × 40″
Brown stripe (border corners, flower centers)	¼ yard	4 squares 6¼″ × 6¼″ 9 Template C
Green mottle (stems, leaves)	⅝ yard	*4 bias strips 1¾″ × 26″ *4 bias strips 1¾″ × 18″ 11 Template D
Gold dot (flower petals)	¼ yard	40 Template B
Gold print (flower petals)	¼ yard	32 Template B
Assorted green prints/textures (leaves)	⅜ yard total	29 Template D total
Backing	3¼ yards	
Batting	Twin size	
OTHER MATERIALS		
⅝″ bias bar (optional)		
Paper-backed fusible web (optional)	3 yards	

*Cut first.

Ann added the daisies using quick fusible appliqué methods. Do likewise if you wish, using a machine buttonhole stitch to secure the edges.

Piecing the Blocks

1. Align the raw edges of a medium blue mottle $1\frac{1}{2}'' \times 8\frac{1}{2}''$ strip with the raw edge of the 90° angle of a cream print $6\frac{7}{8}''$ half-square triangle; stitch the strip to the side of the triangle. In the same manner, align and stitch a blue $1\frac{1}{2}'' \times 9\frac{1}{2}''$ strip to the opposite side. Align a rotary-cutting ruler with the raw edge of the cream triangle and trim away the excess strip length. Make 4 basket tops.

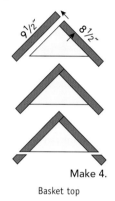

Make 4.

Basket top

2. Sew Template A fabric to the blue $5\frac{7}{8}''$ half-square triangle. Make 4 basket bases.

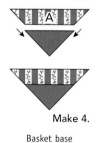

Make 4.

Basket base

3. For the basket side strip, sew a blue $2\frac{7}{8}''$ half-square triangle to cream $2\frac{1}{2}'' \times 6\frac{1}{2}''$ strips. Make 4 of each.

Make 4.

Make 4.

Basket side strips

4. To make the Basket block, refer to the illustration below. Stitch the basket top to the basket bottom. Sew pieced strips to the bottom sides. Add cream $2\frac{1}{2}'' \times 10\frac{1}{2}''$ and $2\frac{1}{2}'' \times 12\frac{1}{2}''$ strips to the top sides. Stitch a cream $4\frac{7}{8}''$ half-square triangle to the corner. Make 4 Basket blocks.

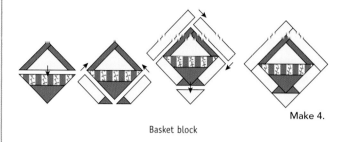

Make 4.

Basket block

Quilt Top Assembly

Refer to the assembly diagram, page 18, for the following steps.

Note: The setting triangles on all edges and corners are cut oversized to allow trimming the quilt edges even after assembly.

1. Arrange and stitch 3 diagonal rows using blocks, light blue print 19″ quarter-square triangles, and a light blue $12\frac{1}{2}''$ square. Sew the rows together. Stitch light blue 10″ half-square triangles to the corners. Trim the quilt edges even.

2. Sew light brown print $1\frac{1}{2}'' \times 40''$ strips to the sides of the quilt; trim even with the top and bottom. Sew the remaining light brown strips to the top/bottom; trim even with the sides.

3. Measure the exact width of the quilt (raw edge to raw edge). Trim 2 blue $6\frac{1}{4}'' \times 40''$ strips to the exact width measurement; sew brown stripe $6\frac{1}{4}''$ squares to the ends of the trimmed strips. Stitch untrimmed blue strips to the sides of the quilt; trim even with the top/bottom. Stitch pieced strips to the top/bottom.

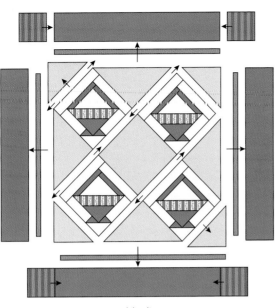

Assembly diagram

Quilting and Finishing

See Basic Quiltmaking Instructions, pages 65–70, for instructions on quilting and binding.

1. Layer and baste the quilt top for the quilting method of your choice. Ann machine quilted. The blocks and appliqués are ditch quilted. Meander quilting covers the cream, light blue, and brown stripe areas. A leaf design is quilted on the outer border, and a single wavy line is stitched along the inner border.

2. Bind the quilt with light brown print fabric.

Appliquéing the Quilt Top

See Basic Quiltmaking Instructions, pages 65–70, for instructions on appliqué.

1. Fold green mottle 1³/₄˝ bias strips in half, wrong sides together. Stitch ¹/₄˝ from the raw edge. Trim the seam allowance to ¹/₈˝. Press the tube flat, centering the seam allowance on the back so the raw edge isn't visible from the front. Using a ⁵/₈˝ bias bar makes pressing faster and easier. Make 8.

Make 8.

Stem bias tube

2. Referring to the quilt photo, page 16, for stem placement, position the prepared stems and trim if needed. Using the appliqué method of your choice, appliqué in place. Position and appliqué, or follow the manufacturer's instruction, to fuse in place all template fabrics to complete the quilt top.

Image of Jakarta

Skill Level 3

Designed by Julie Sheckman.

Finished quilt size: 51½" × 51½"

Number of blocks & finished size:
4 Image of Jakarta blocks 15" × 15"

Journey to a place far away as you piece and appliqué richly colored fabrics together to make this Eastern-influenced wallhanging. Julie's unique appliqué technique makes the trip quick and enjoyable.

Fabric Requirements and Cutting Instructions

FABRIC	AMOUNT	CUTTING
		See the Pullout at the back of the book for template patterns. Appliqué template patterns are printed reversed and without seam allowances.
Dark orange texture (stems, pieced border)	½ yard	*2 strips 1½" × width of fabric (WOF) (pieced border) 32 strips 1" × 5¼" (bias-cut)
Beige texture (appliqué background)	1 yard	16 squares 7½" × 7½"
#1 and #2 red prints (pieced leaves/buds, pieced border)	½ yard each	4 strips 1¾" × WOF (leaves/buds) from each 2 strips 1½" × WOF (pieced border) from each
#3 red print (sashing)	⅜ yard	24 strips 1½" × 7½"
#4 red print (berries, pieced border)	¼ yard	*2 strips 1½" × WOF (pieced border) 16 Template C
#5 red print (pieced border, outer border corners)	⅜ yard	1 strip 1½" × WOF (pieced border) 4 squares 5½" × 5½"
#1 brown print (pieced leaves/buds, sashing posts, pieced border)	½ yard	*4 strips 1¾" × WOF (leaves/buds) *1 strip 1½" × WOF (pieced border) 9 squares 1½" × 1½"
#2 brown print (pieced leaves/buds, pieced border)	½ yard	4 strips 1¾" × WOF (leaves/buds) 2 strips 1½" × WOF (pieced border)
#3 brown print (narrow borders, bias-cut binding)	1¼ yards	6 strips 1½" × WOF (narrow borders, not pieced border) 2 strips 1½" × 45", pieced from 3 WOF strips (narrow border)
#4 and #5 brown prints (pieced border)	¼ yard each	2 strips 1½" × WOF (pieced border) from each
#6 brown print (pieced border, outer border)	1⅜ yards	2 strips 1½" × 45", cut on lengthwise grain (pieced border) 4 strips 5½" × 45", cut on lengthwise grain
Backing	3½ yards	
Batting	Twin size	
OTHER MATERIALS Bias bar, ¼" (optional) Paper-backed fusible web Seam sealant (optional) Mettler Cordonnet thread: brown, burgundy, variegated Size 90/14 or 100/16 sewing machine needle	 1½ yards	

*Cut first.

Julie cut the appliqué leaves and buds from pieced fabric strips and fused the appliqué using Steam-A-Seam 2. She quilted with Mettler Cordonnet thread around the appliqué as a special highlight.

Because the fabric colors are so closely related, we call for red prints #1-5 and brown prints #1-6, plus beige texture and a dark orange texture.

Piecing and Appliquéing the Blocks and Three-Patch Segments

See Basic Quiltmaking Instructions, pages 65–70, for instructions on appliqué.

1. To make stems, fold dark orange texture 1″ × 5¼″ bias strips in half, wrong sides together. Stitch ¼″ from the raw edge. Trim the seam allowance to ⅛″. Press the tube flat, centering the seam allowance on the back so the raw edge isn't visible from the front. Using a ¼″ bias bar makes pressing faster and easier. Make 32.

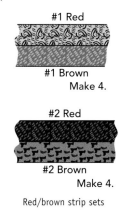

Make 32.

Stem bias tube

2. Trace Templates A–C (including the A and B center line) on the paper side of paper-backed fusible web. Cut apart, leaving a small margin beyond the drawn lines. Following the manufacturer's instructions, fuse the Template C traced circles to the wrong side of #4 red fabric; cut apart on the drawn lines.

3. Sew #1 red and #1 brown 1¾″ × WOF strips together to make strip sets. Make 4. Press the seam allowance open. Repeat using #2 red and #2 brown 1¾″ × WOF strips. Make 4; press open.

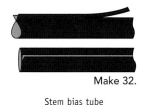

#1 Red

#1 Brown
Make 4.

#2 Red

#2 Brown
Make 4.

Red/brown strip sets

4. Place the #1 strip set **right side down** on the ironing board. Position the traced Template A paper-backed fusible web on the **wrong side** of the strip set, aligning the template center line with the seamline. Following the manufacturer's instructions, fuse and cut apart on the drawn lines. Cut 16 Template A from the #1 strip set combination and 16 from the #2 strip set combination. Repeat this process, fusing and cutting 8 Template B from each strip set combination.
Note: Julie reversed the fabric color direction of the Template B buds for the second block of each set. Do likewise if you wish.

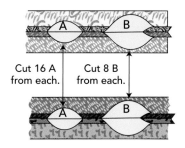

Cut 16 A from each. | Cut 8 B from each.

5. Arrange and sew 3 rows using beige texture 7½″ squares, #3 red 1½″ × 7½″ strips, and #1 brown 1½″ square. Sew the rows together to make pieced background square. Make 4.

Make 4.

Pieced background square

6. Fold the pieced background square in half diagonally twice; use the folds as a placement guide. Referring to the illustration below and the quilt photo, page 20, position the stems, with the raw end abutting the #3 red sashing strip. **Note:** If you're concerned that the stem ends or appliqué edges may fray, apply seam sealant to them, but test a small area first for colorfastness.

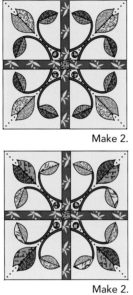

Make 2.

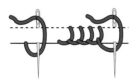

Make 2.

Positioning the appliqué

7. Using a machine or hand buttonhole stitch, appliqué the stems in place. Position the matching pieced Template A, pieced Template B, and Template C fabrics. Following the manufacturer's instructions, fuse in place to make Image of Jakarta blocks. Make 2 blocks of each color combination.

Buttonhole stitch

8. Sew assorted red and assorted brown $1\frac{1}{2}'' \times$ WOF strips together to make the quantities of strip sets indicated below for the pieced border. Press in the direction of the arrows. From each, cut 72 segments $1\frac{1}{2}''$ wide; set aside for the pieced border. **Note:** Julie made strip sets using 2 matching red or 2 matching brown fabric strips for the outer edges of each strip set. Do likewise if you wish.

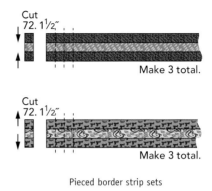

Cut 72. $1\frac{1}{2}''$

Make 3 total.

Cut 72. $1\frac{1}{2}''$

Make 3 total.

Pieced border strip sets

Quilt Top Assembly

Refer to the assembly diagram for the following steps.

1. To make the pieced sashing strip, sew a #1 brown $1\frac{1}{2}''$ square between two #3 red $1\frac{1}{2}'' \times 7\frac{1}{2}''$ strips. Make 4. To make the block rows, sew 2 blocks (using one of each color arrangement per row) and 1 pieced sashing strip together. To make the middle sashing row, sew 2 pieced sashing strips together with a #1 brown $1\frac{1}{2}''$ square in the center. With the sashing row between the block rows, sew the rows together.

2. Sew #3 brown $1\frac{1}{2}'' \times$ WOF strips to the sides; trim even with the top and bottom. Sew #3 brown $1\frac{1}{2}'' \times$ WOF strips to the top/bottom; trim even with the sides.

3. Sew 2 strips of 33 segments (made in Step 8) each, alternating colors. Sew to the sides of the quilt. Stitch 2 strips of 39 segments each and stitch to the top/bottom. Sew #3 brown $1\frac{1}{2}'' \times$ WOF strips to the sides; trim even. Sew the remaining #3 brown strips to the top/bottom; trim even.

4. Measure the exact width of the quilt top (from raw edge to raw edge). Trim two #6 brown $5\frac{1}{2}'' \times 45''$ strips to this measurement and sew #5 red $5\frac{1}{2}''$ squares to the ends. Sew untrimmed #6 brown strips to the sides; trim even. Stitch pieced strips to the top/bottom.

Quilting and Finishing

See Basic Quiltmaking Instructions, pages 65–70, for instructions on quilting and binding.

1. Layer and baste the quilt top for the quilting method of your choice. Julie prefers Hobbs fusible batting and machine quilted around the appliqué in the following manner: Insert a size 90/14 or 100/16 needle into the machine and set the stitch length at approximately 9 stitches per inch. Using brown Mettler Cordonnet thread in the needle and all-purpose thread in the bobbin, stitch next to the Template A edge (burgundy around Template B shapes), leaving enough thread at the beginning and end to pull to back and tie off. For best results, stitch slowly and use an appliqué or open-toe foot. Julie ditch quilted the sashing and added a meander on the background. Using variegated thread, a continuous leaf design was added on the pieced border and a scroll design appears on the #3 brown borders. The outer border is quilted with a continuous undulating loop that forms squares.

2. Bind the quilt with bias-cut #3 brown fabric.

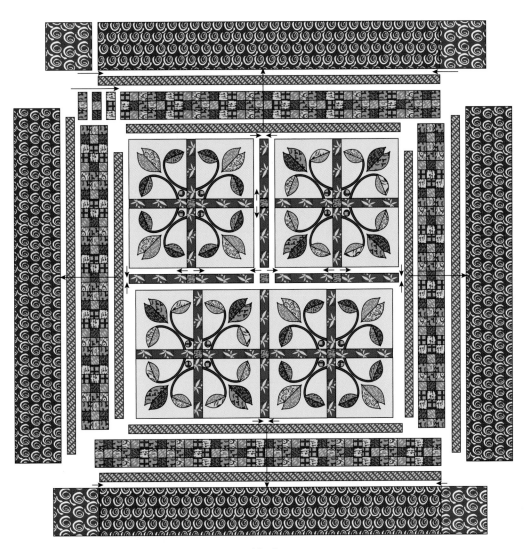

Assembly diagram

Morning Glory

Photographed at Old Glory Antiques,
11825 US Highway 285, Conifer, CO 80433

Skill Level 2

Designed by Kathie Holland.

Made by Kathie Holland and Mary Lowe.

Finished quilt size: 70″ × 78½″

Number of blocks & finished size:
52 Simple Star blocks 6″ × 6″

Flowers scramble up a patchwork trellis, reaching for the springtime sun, in this beautiful quilt.

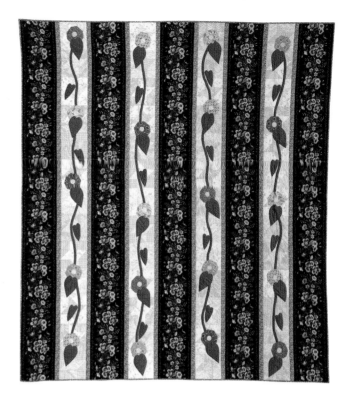

Fabric Requirements and Cutting Instructions

PLANNING

Kathie chose her assorted cream/beige fabrics in similar colors and values to keep the pieced background of the appliqué strips very subtle. Yardage for the brown/pink floral stripe strips is based on the feature fabric, which has five stripe repeats across its width.

FABRIC	AMOUNT	CUTTING
		See the Pullout at the back of the book for template patterns. Appliqué template patterns are printed without seam allowances.
Assorted cream/beige textures, checks and prints (blocks, flower centers)	2¾–3¼ yards total	for stars, cut 52 matching sets of:
		2 squares 2⅞″ × 2⅞″ and
		1 square 2½″ × 2½″
		for star backgrounds, cut 52 matching sets of:
		2 squares 2⅞″ × 2⅞″ and
		4 squares 2½″ × 2½″
		20 Template B total
Green texture (vines, leaves)	1 yard	*1 bias-cut strip 1½″ × 266″
		20 Template C
		8 each Templates D/Dr
Assorted pink prints (flowers)	½–¾ yard total	20 Template A total
Pink small print (narrow strips, binding)	1½ yards	8 strips 1½″ × 82″, pieced from 16 width of fabric (WOF) strips
Brown/pink floral stripe (wide strips)	**2½ yards	**5 strips 8″ × 82″, cut on lengthwise grain
Backing (piece vertically)	5 yards	
Batting	Full/Double size	
OTHER MATERIALS		
Bias bar, ½″ (optional)		
Paper-backed fusible web (optional)	3½ yards	

*Cut first.   **See Planning.

Piecing the Blocks and Appliquéing the Strips

See Basic Quiltmaking Instructions, pages 65–70, for instructions on appliqué.

1. From cream/beige texture fabrics, select 1 set of star background fabric (A) and star fabric (B). On the wrong side of a fabric A 2⅞″ square, draw a diagonal line with the marking tool of your choice. Place the fabric A square on the fabric B 2⅞″ square, right sides together. Sew a ¼″ seam on each side of the marked line; cut apart on the marked line. Press open to make pieced squares. Make 52 sets of 4 matching.

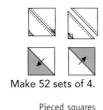

Make 52 sets of 4.

Pieced squares

2. Using matching 2½″ squares and pieced squares, arrange and sew 3 rows. Sew the rows together to complete Simple Star blocks. Make 52 total.

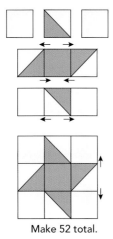

Make 52 total.

Simple Star block

3. Referring to the quilt photo, page 25, and the assembly diagram, sew 13 blocks together to make a pieced strip. Make 4 total.

4. To make vines, fold a green texture bias-cut 1½″ × 266″ strip in half, wrong sides together. Stitch ¼″ from the raw edge. Trim the seam allowance to ⅛″. Press the tube flat, centering the seam allowance on the back so the raw edge isn't visible from the front. Using a ½″ bias bar makes pressing faster and easier. Cut the strip into 16 lengths 10″–16″ each.

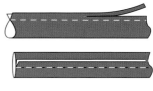

Vine bias tube

5. Referring to the quilt photo, page 25, position the vine segments on the pieced strips. You may want to temporarily arrange your Template A and C fabrics on top of the vine segments to ensure a pleasing design. **Note:** Kathie and Mary started and ended each vine at slightly different places on the strips, to give the quilt a more natural garden appearance. Trim the vine segments as needed. Using the appliqué method of your choice, appliqué the vines in place. Add Template A–D fabrics in alphabetical order and appliqué in place.

Quilt Top Assembly

Refer to the assembly diagram for the following steps.

Sew pink small-print 1½″ × 82″ strips to the sides of the pieced/appliquéd strips; trim the top and bottom even. Sew brown/pink floral stripe strips and pieced/appliquéd strips together, alternating. Trim the top/bottom even.

Quilting and Finishing

See Basic Quiltmaking Instructions, pages 65–70, for instructions on quilting and binding.

1. Layer and baste the quilt top for the quilting method of your choice. Kathie and Mary used Mountain Mist Cream Rose batting and machine quilted. Strips and appliqués were stitched in the ditch, and a staggered double cable fills the brown floral strips.

2. Bind the quilt with pink small-print fabric.

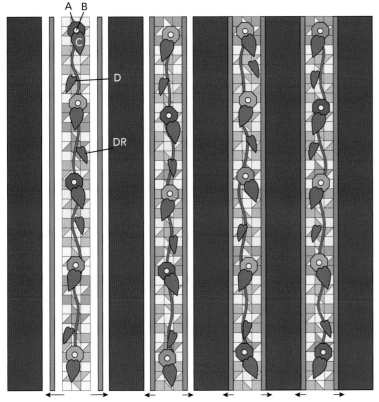

Assembly diagram

Sweetheart Stars

Skill Level 3

Designed by Vicki Hoskins.

Machine quilted by Jane Ann Houser.

Finished quilt size: 51″ × 51″

Number of blocks & finished size:
9 Lattice Star blocks 9″ × 9″

Romantic, yes, but men like it too! Say "I love you" with this just-sweet-enough treat.

Fabric Requirements and Cutting Instructions

PLANNING

This quilt has such a sweet appeal. The strips for the vines are cut on the bias.

FABRIC	AMOUNT	CUTTING
		See the Pullout at the back of the book for template patterns. Appliqué template patterns are printed without seam allowances. Piecing template patterns are printed with seam allowances.
Medium pink texture (blocks, buds, narrow border)	$1^3/8$ yards	*4 strips 1″ × 44″, cut on lengthwise grain 36 squares $2^3/8$″ × $2^3/8$″, cut in half diagonally to make 72 half-square triangles 18 squares $2^3/8$″ × $2^3/8$″ 8 Template B
Burgundy texture (blocks, flower centers)	$5/8$ yard	36 each Templates A/Ar 8 Template D
Cherry red texture (blocks)	$1/4$ yard	9 squares $4^1/4$″ × $4^1/4$″, cut in half twice diagonally to make 36 quarter-square triangles
Black solid (blocks, vines, leaves, narrow border, binding)	$1^3/8$ yards	*4 strips $3/4$″ × 45″, cut on lengthwise grain 18 squares $2^3/8$″ × $2^3/8$″ **1 bias-cut strip $1^1/4$″ × 130″ 36 Template B
Red paisley (blocks, buds, outer border)	$1^3/4$ yards	*4 strips $6^1/2$″ × 57″, cut on lengthwise grain 72 squares 2″ × 2″ 9 squares $3^1/2$″ × $3^1/2$″ 16 Template B
White solid (blocks, inner border)	$1^3/8$ yards	*4 strips $5^1/2$″ × 43″, cut on lengthwise grain 36 rectangles 2″ × $3^1/2$″
Red/cream print (blocks, flowers)	$3/8$ yard	36 squares 2″ × 2″ 8 Template C
Backing	$3^3/8$ yards	
Batting	Twin size	

OTHER MATERIALS

Bias bar, $3/8$″ (optional)

*Cut first.   **See Planning.

Piecing the Blocks

1. Sew medium pink texture $2\frac{3}{8}$" half-square triangles, Template A and Ar fabrics, and a cherry red texture $4\frac{1}{4}$" quarter-square triangle together to make a pieced rectangle. Make 36.

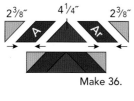

Make 36.

Pieced rectangle

2. On the wrong side of a pink $2\frac{3}{8}$" square, draw a diagonal line with the marking tool of your choice. Place the pink square on a black $2\frac{3}{8}$" square, right sides together. Sew a $\frac{1}{4}$" seam on each side of the marked line; cut apart on the marked line. Press open to make pieced squares. Make 36.

Make 36.

Pieced squares

3. Draw a diagonal line on the wrong side of a red paisley 2" square. Place the red square on a white 2" × $3\frac{1}{2}$" rectangle, right sides together, aligning the raw edges. Stitch on the drawn line; trim away and discard the excess fabric. Press open. Repeat on the opposite end of the white rectangle to make flying geese units. Make 36.

Make 36.

Flying geese unit

4. Arrange and sew 3 rows using pieced squares, flying geese units, and a red paisley $3\frac{1}{2}$" square. Sew the rows together to make block centers. Press seams open. Make 9.

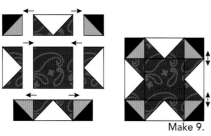

Make 9.

Block center

5. Arrange and sew 3 rows using red/cream print 2" squares, pieced rectangles, and a block center. Sew the rows together to complete Lattice Star blocks. Make 9.

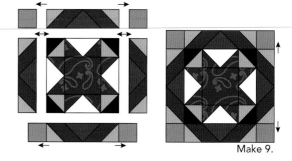

Make 9.

Lattice Star block

Quilt Top Assembly and Appliqué

Refer to the assembly diagram for the following steps. See Basic Quiltmaking Instructions, pages 65–70, for instructions on appliqué.

1. Stitch 3 rows of 3 blocks each. Sew the rows together. Press seams open.
2. Fold a white $5\frac{1}{2}$" × 43" strip in half; press the fold. In the same manner, fold and press a pink 1" × 44" strip, a black $\frac{3}{4}$" × 45" strip, and a red paisley $6\frac{1}{2}$" × 57" strip. Open the folds and sew the strips together, matching the fold lines. Make 4.

Align folds.

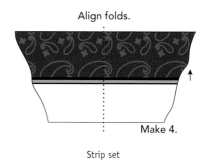

Make 4.

Strip set

3. Finger-press the quilt top in half lengthwise and crosswise; use the folds as placement lines. Pin the prepared border strips to the sides of the quilt, matching the center fold lines. Starting and stopping $\frac{1}{4}$" from the quilt corners, sew the pieced borders to all 4 sides of the quilt. Sew and trim miters. Press seams open.

4. To make vines, fold a black bias-cut 1¼″ × 130″ strip in half, wrong sides together. Stitch ¼″ from the raw edge. Trim the seam allowance to ⅛″. Press the tube flat, centering the seam allowance on the back so the raw edge isn't visible from the front. Using a ⅜″ bias bar makes pressing faster and easier. Cut the strip into 8 lengths 15″ each.

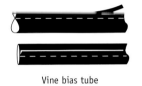

Vine bias tube

5. Referring to the quilt photo, page 29, position the vines on the white border. Using the appliqué method of your choice, appliqué in place. Add Template B–D fabrics and appliqué in place.

Quilting and Finishing

See Basic Quiltmaking Instructions, pages 65–70, for instructions on quilting and binding.

1. Layer and baste the quilt top for the quilting method of your choice. Jane Ann machine quilted an overall feathered pattern in the quilt center and outer border. She outline stitched the appliqué and filled the white border with an echo-quilted floral pattern.

2. Bind the quilt with black solid fabric.

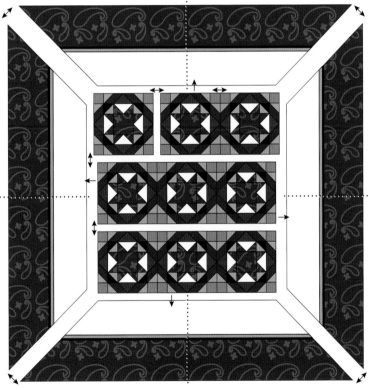

Assembly diagram

Cozy Afternoon

Designed by Lisa DeBee Schiller.

Finished sizes:

Tea Cozy 10$\frac{1}{4}$" × 14"

Teacup Cozy 6$\frac{1}{2}$" × 9"

Share secrets and swap stories with a friend over your favorite pot of tea. Lisa DeBee Schiller's pretty posy cozies will keep everything warm while you catch up on each other's adventures. Felted wool is a natural insulator and a unique update on an old-fashioned nicety.

Fabric Requirements and Cutting Instructions

The felted wool and batting used in these cozies will help keep your tea service piping hot. If you're felting your own wool, machine wash and dry on high heat settings, repeating until fabric "felts up." You can also purchase prefelted wool at most quilt shops.

FABRIC	AMOUNT	CUTTING
Makes 1 tea cozy and 2 teacup cozies.		*See the Pullout at the back of the book for template patterns. Appliqué template patterns are printed without seam allowances. Piecing template patterns are printed with seam allowances.*
Pale pink felted wool	6" × 12" piece	1 Template A
Olive green felted wool	5" × 10" piece	1 Template B
Light green felted wool	3" × 6" piece	1 Template C
Dark green felted wool	5" × 11" piece	1 Template D
Medium green felted wool	11" × 12" piece	1 Template E
		2 Template P
Dark purple felted wool	6" × 6" piece	14 Template F
Medium purple felted wool	6" × 6" piece	14 Template G
Light purple felted wool	7" × 7" piece	7 Template H
Light gold felted wool	5" × 5" piece	7 Template I
White felted wool	5" × 6" piece	1 each Templates J/Jr and K
Medium pink felted wool	7" × 12" piece	2 each Templates L and M
Rose felted wool	3" × 5" piece	2 Template N
Tan felted wool	4" × 5" piece	2 Template O
Dusty green felted wool (front/back, tea cozy)	16" × 24" piece	2 Template Q
Pale peach and pale yellow felted wool (fronts, teacup cozies)	8" × 11" piece each	1 each Template R
Ecru/lavender print (tea cozy lining, binding)	$\frac{1}{2}$ yard	*1 square 12" × 12"
		2 Template Q
Green/peach print and rose print (teacup cozy backs, binding)	$\frac{3}{8}$ yard each	*1 square 10" × 10" from each
		1 each Template R
Ecru/rose print (teacup cozy linings)	$\frac{1}{4}$ yard	4 Template R
Batting (low-loft)	22" × 30" piece	2 Template Q
		4 Template R
OTHER MATERIALS		
Embroidery floss, rose variegated		

See Planning, page 34.

PLANNING

Lisa's cozies are finished with bias binding made from fabric squares. Use 1¼″ for binding strip width when marking the pieced parallelograms.

Adding the Appliqué

See Basic Quiltmaking Instructions, pages 65–70, for instructions on appliqué.

1. Position Template A–P fabrics on 1 Template Q and both Template R wool fabrics.

Make 1.

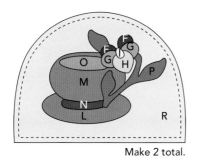

Make 2 total.

2. Using the appliqué method of your choice, appliqué in place. Lisa did raw-edge appliqué using a hand buttonhole stitch.

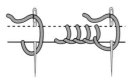

Buttonhole stitch

3. Using rose variegated embroidery floss in stem stitch, add teacup details (see Templates M and O).

Teacup details

Quilting and Finishing

See Basic Quiltmaking Instructions, pages 65–70, for instructions on quilting and binding.

1. Layer and baste the cozy fronts and backs for the quilting method of your choice. Lisa hand quilted around the pale pink glove on the tea cozy front and added the word "Tea" to its back. The teacup cozies were not quilted.

2. Layer the tea cozy front and back, lining sides together, aligning the raw edges. Bind the curved edge with ecru/lavender print bias binding, sewing through all layers. Trim the binding even with the cozy bottom. Finish the bottom edge of the cozy with ecru/lavender bias binding.

3. Layer Template R shapes as follows: green/peach print, right side down; batting; ecru/rose print, right side up; ecru/rose print, right side down; batting; pale peach appliquéd front, right side up. Bind the curved edge with green/peach bias binding; trim even. Bind the bottom, taking care to keep the front 3 layers separate from the back layers. Using the remaining Template R shapes, pale yellow appliquéd front, and rose print binding, make the remaining teacup cozy.

Climbing Garden

Photographed at Scandinavian Designs,
9000 E. Hampden Avenue., Denver, CO 80231;
www.ScandinavianDesigns.com

Skill Level 2

Designed by Ann Weber.

Finished quilt size: 56½" × 64½"

A simple but effective pieced border gives this strippy appliquéd beauty some extra pizzazz. Beginning to intermediate quilters will welcome the fast construction and the opportunity to practice their appliqué method of choice.

Fabric Requirements and Cutting Instructions

Accurate ¼" seams are essential in piecing the outer borders to achieve the perfect frame effect of Ann's design. However, if your pieced strips are off by just a bit, the corner flower appliqués can be arranged to help hide small errors! Ann arranged four of her darkest assorted red flowers for the corner appliqués; you may wish to do the same.

FABRIC	AMOUNT	CUTTING
		See the Pullout at the back of the book for template patterns. Appliqué template patterns are printed without seam allowances.
Green paisley print (vines)	⅝ yard	1 bias-cut strip 1½" × 195"
Beige texture	1¾ yards	2 strips 11½" × 56", cut on lengthwise grain
Cream texture	1¾ yards	1 strip 11½" × 56", cut on lengthwise grain
Assorted green prints and textures (leaves)	¼–½ yard total	30 Template A total
Assorted red prints and textures (large flowers)	⅝–1 yard total	13 sets of 6 matching Template B
Assorted gold prints and textures (flower centers)	⅛–¼ yard total	9 sets of 3 matching Template E 13 Template C total
Rose print (small flowers)	*1 fat quarter	15 Template D
Pink print (small flowers)	*1 fat quarter	12 Template D
Light green leaf print (strips)	1⅝ yards	4 strips 4½" × 54½", cut on lengthwise grain
Green dot (border)	⅜ yard	2 strips 1½" × 54½", pieced from 3 width of fabric (WOF) strips 2 strips 1½" × 48½", pieced from 3 WOF strips
Rose floral (pieced border)	⅝ yard	7 squares 9¼" × 9¼", cut in half twice diagonally to make 28 quarter-square triangles (2 left over)
Beige/rose print (pieced border)	¾ yard	6 squares 9¼" × 9¼", cut in half twice diagonally to make 24 quarter-square triangles (2 left over) 4 squares 4⅞" × 4⅞", cut in half diagonally to make 8 half-square triangles 4 squares 4½" × 4½"
Dark green texture (binding)	¾ yard	
Backing (piece horizontally)	3¾ yards	
Batting	Twin size	
OTHER MATERIALS		
Bias bar, ½" (optional)		

A fat quarter is an 18" × 20–22" cut of fabric or a true quarter of a yard.

Appliquéing and Piecing the Quilt Center

See Basic Quiltmaking Instructions, pages 65–70, for instructions on appliqué.

1. To make vines, fold a green paisley print $1\frac{1}{2}$″ × 195″ bias-cut strip in half, wrong sides together. Stitch $\frac{1}{4}$″ from the raw edge. Trim the seam allowance to $\frac{1}{8}$″. Press the tube flat, centering the seam allowance on the back so the raw edge isn't visible from the front. Using a $\frac{1}{2}$″ bias bar makes pressing faster and easier. Cut the strip into 3 lengths 65″ each.

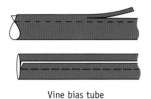

Vine bias tube

2. Referring to the assembly diagram and the quilt photo, position the vines and Template A–E fabrics as shown, in alphabetical order, on beige and cream texture $11\frac{1}{2}$″ × 56″ strips. Keep in mind that the strips will be trimmed to $10\frac{1}{2}$″ × $54\frac{1}{2}$″ (finished size is 10″ × 54″). Using the appliqué method of your choice, appliqué in place. Trim the strips to $10\frac{1}{2}$″ × $54\frac{1}{2}$″.
3. Arrange and stitch light green leaf print $4\frac{1}{2}$″ × $54\frac{1}{2}$″ strips and appliquéd strips together, alternating.

Quilt Top Assembly and Corner Appliqué

Refer to the assembly diagram for the following steps.

1. Sew green dot $1\frac{1}{2}$″ × $54\frac{1}{2}$″ strips to sides; trim even with top/bottom. Sew remaining green dot strips to top/bottom; trim even with sides.
2. Arrange and sew together 7 rose floral $9\frac{1}{4}$″ quarter-square triangles, 6 beige/rose print $9\frac{1}{4}$″ quarter-square triangles, and 2 beige/rose $4\frac{7}{8}$″ half-square triangles to make a side pieced border strip. Make 2. In the same manner, arrange and sew together 6 rose floral and 5 beige/rose quarter-square triangles and 2 beige/rose half-square triangles to make the top/bottom pieced border strip. Make 2.

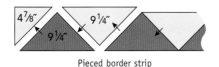

Pieced border strip

3. Sew the side pieced border strips to the sides. Sew beige/rose print $4\frac{1}{2}$″ squares to the ends of the top/bottom border strips; sew the strips to the top and bottom.
4. Referring to the quilt photo, arrange Template A–C fabrics at each corner of the quilt; appliqué in place.

Assembly diagram

Quilting and Finishing

See Basic Quiltmaking Instructions, pages 65–70, for instructions on quilting and binding.

1. Layer and baste the quilt top for the quilting method of your choice. Ann machine quilted, outlining the appliqué and ditch quilting the green border. The wide strips and pieced border are filled with a meander, and the narrow strips with feather bands.
2. Bind the quilt with dark green texture fabric.

Cottage Wreaths

Photographed at Echter's Greenhouse and Gardens,
5150 Garrison Street, Arvada, CO 80002

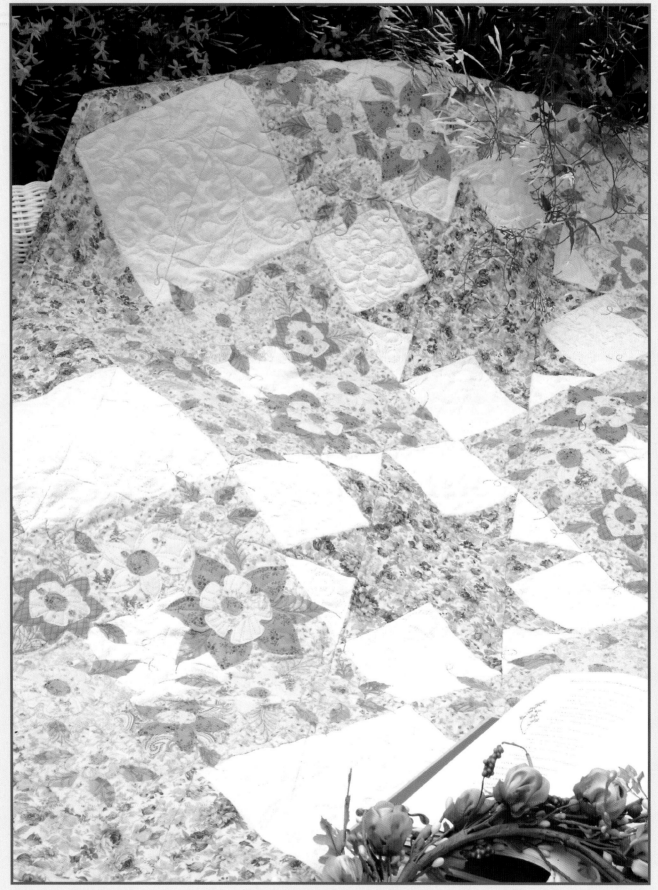

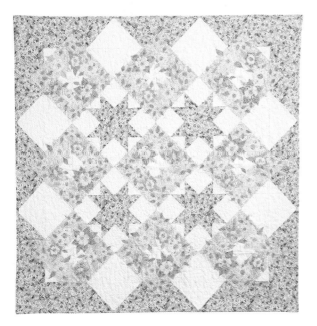

Skill Level 3

Designed by Gerri Robinson.

Machine quilted by Deborah A. Hobbs, Ta Dah Custom Longarm Quilting.

Finished quilt size: 60½″ × 60½″

Number of blocks & finished size:
64 assorted square blocks 6″ × 6″

Appliquéd flowers scattered over pieced blocks that feature dainty floral prints lend cottage-style charm to this pretty quilt.

Fabric Requirements and Cutting Instructions

Gerri's intriguing patchwork design is made up of simple pieced squares sewn together in horizontal rows! All pieced squares are constructed using a simple "corner sew and clip" technique.

The appliqués on the featured quilt were added with a light fusible web after the quilt top was assembled. Quilting secures the appliqués in place and adds a lovely texture to the quilt. We provide step-by-step instructions for Gerri's speedy one-step appliqué method on page 41.

FABRIC	AMOUNT	CUTTING
		See the Pullout at the back of the book for template patterns. Appliqué template patterns are printed reversed and without seam allowances.
Light blue floral	2 yards	36 squares 6½″ × 6½″ 48 squares 3½″ × 3½″ 12 rectangles 3½″ × 6½″
Cream texture	2⅛ yards	72 squares 3½″ × 3½″ 24 squares 6½″ × 6½″ 8 rectangles 6½″ × 12½″
Multicolored floral (stars, border, binding)	2½ yards	56 squares 3½″ × 3½″ 24 squares 6½″ × 6½″ 20 rectangles 3½″ × 6½″
Assorted green florals (leaves)	¾–1 yard total	27 Template A total 45 Template B total 180 Template C total
Assorted rose textures (flowers, flower centers)	¾–1 yard total	9 each Templates D, I, J, and L total 36 each Templates G and P total
Assorted yellow florals (flowers)	1–1¼ yards total	9 each Templates D, I, K, L, and M total 18 Template F total 36 Template O total
Assorted pink florals (flowers)	1 yard total	18 each Templates E and H total 9 Template M total 36 Template N total
Backing	4 yards	
Batting	Twin size	
OTHER MATERIALS		
Paper-backed fusible web, lightweight	8 yards	

Piecing the Blocks and Border Elements

1. Draw a diagonal line on the wrong side of a cream 3½" square with the marking tool of your choice. Place a cream square on a light blue 6½" square, right sides together, aligning the raw edges. Stitch on the drawn line; trim away and discard the excess fabric. Press open. Repeat this process on the opposite corner to make a pieced square. Make 36.

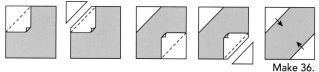

Pieced square 1

Make 36.

2. Repeat the mark, stitch, trim, and press process using 2 light blue 3½" squares on a cream 6½" square, as shown below. Make 8.

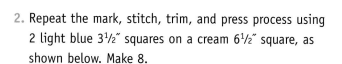

Pieced square 2

Make 8.

3. In the same manner, use 2 light blue and 2 multicolored floral 3½" squares on a cream 6½" square. Make 16.

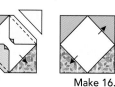

Pieced square 3

Make 16.

4. Again repeat the mark, stitch, trim, and press process using multicolored floral 3½" squares on a light blue 3½" × 6½" rectangle. Make 12 pieced rectangles. In the same manner, make 8 large pieced rectangles using multicolored floral 6½" squares on a cream texture 6½" × 12½" rectangle.

Make 12.   Make 8.

Pieced rectangle

5. Stitch a multicolored floral 3½" × 6½" rectangle to a small pieced rectangle from Step 4. Make 12 for the border.

Make 12.

Pieced border unit

Quilt Top Assembly

Refer to the assembly diagram for the following steps.

1. Using assorted pieced square blocks and multicolored floral 6½" squares, stitch 8 rows of 8 squares each, carefully arranging and rotating the blocks to match the featured quilt. Sew the rows together.

2. Stitch 4 border strips using 2 multicolored floral 3½" × 6½" rectangles, 3 pieced squares (from Step 5), and 2 large pieced rectangles each. Sew 2 strips to the sides of the quilt. Stitch multicolored floral 6½" squares to the ends of the remaining strips and sew to the top and bottom of the quilt.

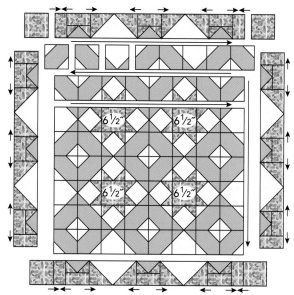

Assembly diagram

Adding the Appliqué

See Basic Quiltmaking Instructions, pages 65–70, for instructions on appliqué.

1. To learn Gerri's method for fusible appliqué, refer to the special instructions (right). Trace Templates A–P on the paper side of paper-backed fusible web. Cut apart, leaving a small margin beyond the drawn lines. Following the manufacturer's instructions, fuse to the wrong side of the appropriate fabrics; cut apart on the drawn lines.

2. Arrange appliqué fabrics on blue "frames." Following the manufacturer's instructions, fuse in place. **Note:** Appliqués are secured with quilting (see below).

Quilting and Finishing

See Basic Quiltmaking Instructions, pages 65–70, for instructions on quilting and binding.

1. Layer and baste the quilt top for the quilting method of your choice. Machine quilt the appliqués in place by stitching close to the edge of each appliqué. Add detail lines and echo quilt as desired. On the featured quilt, green thread was used for the leaf vein lines, and curlicue vines extend from select leaves. A flowing feather appears in each large cream square, and a flower motif is quilted in each small cream square. A meandering floral design is stitched in the multicolored floral areas.

2. Bind the quilt with multicolored floral fabric.

Quilting/appliqué detail

Gerri's Method for All-in-One Appliqué and Quilting

To speed up the quiltmaking process, I secure the appliqués as part of the quilting.

1. Prepare the appliqué fabrics with a light fusible web, following the manufacturer's instructions. I prefer Lite Steam-A-Seam 2. Cut out the appliqués.

2. Arrange the appliqués as desired on your pieced quilt top, layering to create complete flower motifs. In each blue frame, I used approximately 3 A, 5 B, and 20 C for leaves. For flowers I used 2 D/E/F/G arrangements, 1 H/I/J (rotate I so H and I leaves alternate), 1 H/I/K (rotate I), 2 L/M/G, and 4 N/O/P per blue frame.

3. When you're satisfied with the appliqué arrangements, fuse in place following the manufacturer's instructions.

4. Layer and baste the quilt top for quilting. Quilt just inside the appliqué edges to secure. Add more quilting as desired.

A Thoroughly Modern Mary

Fabric Requirements and Cutting Instructions

Jan Carlson, co-founder and former president of the Baltimore Appliqué Society, challenged herself and friend Pat Sloan to create a modern project using a block (below) from Mary Mannakee's famous Baltimore Album quilt, page 45. Here are their results! What a great example of each quiltmaker's personal style shining through, even when the challenge involved just one block design.

Jan's bright version is patterned here. Pat's version is on page 44.

Skill Level 2

Antique quilt owned by Daughters of the American Revolution Museum.

Modern versions made by Jan Carlson and Pat Sloan.

Finished quilt size: 27$\frac{1}{2}$″ × 27$\frac{1}{2}$″

Number of blocks & finished size:
1 Mary Mannakee block 16″ × 16″

The original Mary Mannakee quilt, made circa 1850, was the inspiration for these contemporary wallhangings by Jan Carlson and Pat Sloan. Since its arrival at the Daughters of the American Revolution (DAR) Museum in 1945, the quilt has been restored, patterned, and copied many times over. Mary's legacy lives on, in every new project sparked by her Baltimore Album classic.

FABRIC	AMOUNT	CUTTING
		See the Pullout at the back of the book for template patterns. Appliqué template patterns are printed without seam allowances.
Red/orange mottle (background, berries)	$\frac{5}{8}$ yard	*1 square 18″ × 18″ 24 Template H 12 Template I
Blue stripe (flowers)	9″ × 14″ piece	4 Template A
Orange small print (flower centers)	5″ × 7″ piece	4 Template B
Green/black large dot (flower bases)	9″ × 9″ piece	4 Template C
Green check (leaves, berry caps)	$\frac{1}{4}$ yard	32 Template D 12 Template J
Green/black stripe (vines)	$\frac{7}{8}$ yard	4 Template E 2 each Template G/Gr
Black/orange dot (appliqué center)	9″ × 9″ piece	1 Template F
Green/black medium dot (inner border, binding)	$\frac{1}{2}$ yard	4 strips 1″ × 20″
Black solid (outer border)	$\frac{5}{8}$ yard	*2 strips 5$\frac{1}{2}$″ × 32″ 2 strips 5$\frac{1}{2}$″ × 20″
Blue mottle (berries)	5″ × 5″ piece	8 Template H
Backing	1 yard	
Batting	Crib size	

*Cut first.

Appliquéing the Block

See Basic Quiltmaking Instructions, pages 65–70, for instructions on appliqué.

Finger-press a red/orange mottle 18˝ square in half on both length and width and on both diagonals; use the folds as placement guides. Position Template A–F fabrics (in alphabetical order). Using the appliqué method of your choice, appliqué in place. Trim to 16½˝ square.

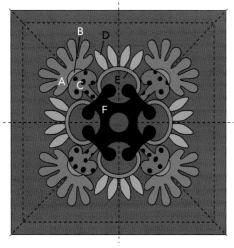

Positioning the appliqué

Pat pieced her appliqué background from four 9˝ squares of assorted brown texture fabrics, then appliquéd using a machine buttonhole stitch and trimmed the quilt center to 16½˝ square before adding the borders and border appliqué. She also cut a circle for the center of the appliqué from a contrasting fabric, instead of trimming it away to expose the background as Jan did. Feel free to play with design decisions like these when you work on your own version.

Quilt Top Assembly and Border Appliqué

Refer to the assembly diagram for the following steps.

1. Stitch a green/black 1˝ × 20˝ strip to each side; trim even with the top and bottom. Stitch the remaining green/black strips to the top/bottom; trim even with the sides. Sew black 5½˝ × 20˝ strips to the sides; trim even. Sew the remaining black strips to the top/bottom; trim even.
2. Referring to the quilt photo, page 42, position Template G–J fabrics and the remaining Template D leaves on the outer border. Appliqué in place.

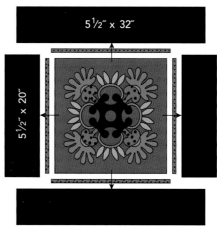

5½˝ x 32˝

5½˝ x 20˝

Assembly diagram

Quilting and Finishing

See Basic Quiltmaking Instructions, pages 65–70, for instructions on quilting and binding.

Layer, baste, and quilt. Jan hand quilted around the appliqué, then filled the background with straight lines ½˝ apart, radiating from the quilt center. Bind with green/black dot fabric.

The fourth block in the third row of this historic quilt served as the starting point for Jan and Pat's mutual challenge.

The Baltimore Appliqué Society

The enduring appeal of Baltimore Album quilts and the need to continue their traditions brought about the founding of the nonprofit Baltimore Appliqué Society in 1993. Centered around Baltimore, where the first of these magnificent quilts was made over 150 years ago, the society's members came together to advance two goals.

The Baltimore Appliqué society (BAS) supports the preservation of quilts, textiles, and related documents in museum and historical society collections, such as original album quilts at the Maryland Historical Society (MHS), National Society Daughters of the American Revolution (NSDAR) Museum, and the Baltimore Museum of Art (BMA). That support includes financial contributions, quilts made as fund-raisers, and hands-on conservation work.

BAS also promotes the art of appliqué and quilting perfected by Baltimore women and revived in the 1980s. In teaching these skills and encouraging each other's work, modern appliqué quiltmakers extend the Baltimore legacy with new colors, designs, and construction techniques.

If you are interested in becoming a member please visit the BAS website: www.baltimoreapplique.com.
The story of the Mary Mannakee quilt is available at this link: www.baltimoreapplique.com/mannakee.html.

All About Autumn

Skill Level 3

Designed by Ann Weber.

Finished quilt size: $48^{1}/_{2}'' \times 48^{1}/_{2}''$

Number of blocks & finished size:
16 Lattice blocks 12″ × 12″

What says autumn better than crisp, colorful leaves? Welcome guests with these lovely wreaths in fall foliage colors. The woven background design will add a new technique to your piecing skills.

Fabric Requirements and Cutting Instructions

FABRIC	AMOUNT	CUTTING
		See the Pullout at the back of the book for template patterns. Appliqué template patterns are printed without seam allowances.
Yellow texture (piecing)	$1^{5}/_{8}$ yards	*8 strips $3^{7}/_{8}'' \times$ width of fabric (WOF) *8 strips $2^{1}/_{4}'' \times$ WOF 16 squares $2^{1}/_{4}'' \times 2^{1}/_{4}''$
Green leaf print (piecing, binding)	$1^{3}/_{8}$ yards	*4 strips $2^{1}/_{4}'' \times$ WOF 32 strips $2^{1}/_{4}'' \times 7^{3}/_{8}''$
Rust print (piecing)	$^{7}/_{8}$ yard	*4 strips $2^{1}/_{4}'' \times$ WOF 32 strips $2^{1}/_{4}'' \times 7^{3}/_{8}''$
Orange print (appliqué)	**1 fat quarter	13 Template A
Orange texture (appliqué)	1 fat quarter	15 Template A
Orange marble (appliqué)	1 fat quarter	12 Template A
#1 Green print (appliqué)	1 fat quarter	16 Template B
#2 Green print (appliqué)	1 fat quarter	16 Template B
#1 Green texture (appliqué)	1 fat quarter	32 Template C
#2 Green texture (appliqué)	1 fat quarter	32 Template C
Backing	$3^{1}/_{4}$ yards	
Batting	Twin size	

Cut first.

**A fat quarter is an 18″ × 20–22″ cut of fabric or a true quarter of a yard.*

Piecing the Blocks

1. Sew the strip sets, press, and cut the segments as shown.

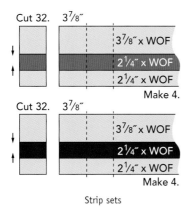

Strip sets

2. Stitch the strips to the sides of the segments in the color arrangements and quantities shown below.

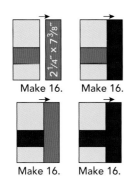

Make 16. Make 16.

Make 16. Make 16.

3. Refer to the illustration below and follow the instructions in Partial Seaming Construction, page 49, to assemble the Lattice blocks. Make 16.

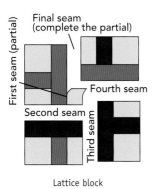

Lattice block

Quilt Top Assembly and Appliqué

Refer to the assembly diagram for the following steps. See Basic Quiltmaking Instructions, pages 65–70, for instructions on appliqué.

1. Stitch 4 rows of 4 blocks each. Stitch the rows together.
2. Referring to the quilt photo, page 46, position Template A–C fabrics. Appliqué in place.

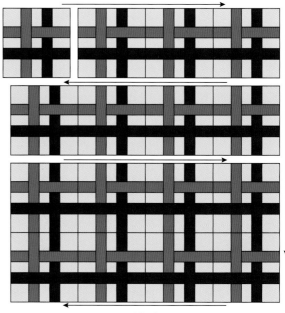

Assembly diagram

Quilting and Finishing

See Basic Quiltmaking Instructions, pages 65–70, for instructions on quilting and binding.

Layer, baste, and quilt. Each green and rust strip is machine quilted with two parallel lines, further emphasizing the woven look. Leaves feature vein details, and the background is filled with a continuous swirl pattern. Bind with green leaf print.

Partial Seaming Construction

Ann's blocks get their woven look from partial seaming construction. The photographs show you step-by-step how to assemble the components of this intriguing block.

1. Align the raw edges of a yellow $2\frac{1}{4}''$ square with the corner of a pieced rectangle, right sides together. Sew a partial seam, starting approximately 1" from the top of the $2\frac{1}{4}''$ square.

2. Open out the yellow square and press the partial seam.

3–6. Sew the second, third, and fourth pieced rectangles to the first unit.

7. Finish sewing the partial seam, continuing the seam to join the fourth rectangle to the first.

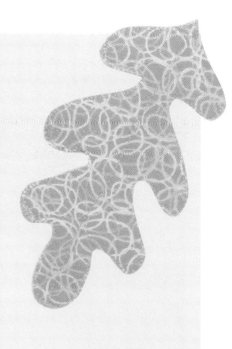

Wool Etchings

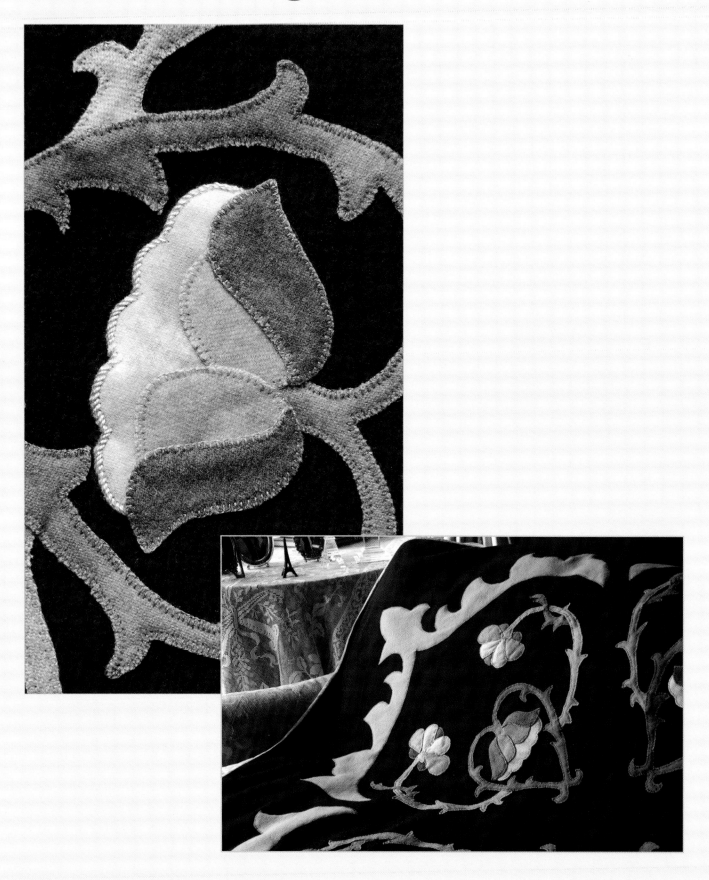

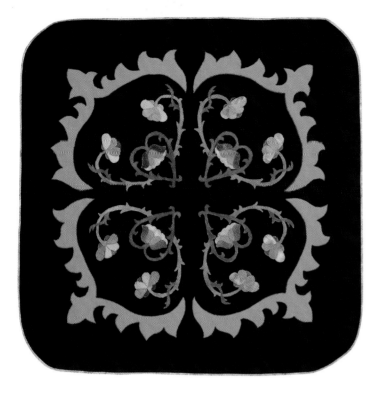

Skill Level

Designed by Paula Kanner.

Finished throw size: 57″ × 57″

Keep cozy and warm under this beautiful all-wool throw. Gorgeous hand-dyed woolens give these blossoms and stems lifelike appeal.

Fabric Requirements and Cutting Instructions

The wool hand-dying process creates the lovely variations in shade and color seen here and felts the fabric at the same time. Wool and quilt shops—and even some fabric stores—are good sources for hand-dyed woolens. To felt wool, wash and dry on high heat settings, cleaning lint traps often. The felting process causes the wool to shrink, so be sure to purchase larger than felted size.

FABRIC	AMOUNT	CUTTING
		See the Pullout at the back of the book for template patterns. Appliqué template patterns are printed without seam allowances.
Black coat-weight wool, unfelted (background)	57″ × 57″ piece	
Dark rose hand-dyed wool	15″ × 15″ piece	8 Template A
		4 each Template H/Hr
Light green hand-dyed wool	20″ × 24″ piece	4 each Template B/Br
Medium green hand-dyed wool	24″ × 25″ piece	4 each Template C/Cr
		4 Template F
Medium rose hand-dyed wool	12″ × 13″ piece	24 Template D
Light rose hand-dyed wool	11″ × 17″ piece	16 Template E
		4 Template G
Light green felted wool (scrollwork border)	34″ × 56″ piece	4 Template I
Rose batik (woven cotton bias-cut binding)	¾ yard	
OTHER MATERIALS		
Paper-backed fusible web (optional)	2½ yards	
#5 or #8 perle cotton or embroidery floss		

Appliquéing the Throw

See Basic Quiltmaking Instructions, pages 65–70, for instructions on appliqué.

1. Using light-colored thread, baste a black 57″ square along the midlines, lengthwise and widthwise, and on both diagonals; use the basting lines as a placement guide.
2. Position Template A–I fabrics.

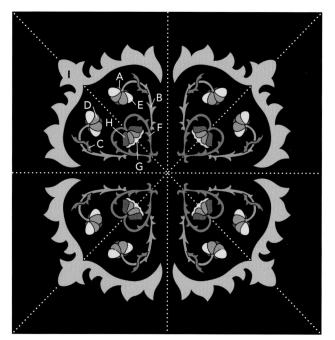

Positioning the appliqué

3. Appliqué in place using matching perle cotton or embroidery floss with a hand buttonhole stitch.

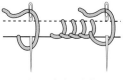

Buttonhole stitch

Note: Paula used fusible web to stabilize the stem and flower template fabrics during appliqué. To avoid stiffness, she did not use fusible web for the large scrollwork border pieces. If using fusible web, trace Templates A–H on the paper side of web. Cut apart, leaving a small margin beyond the drawn line. Following the manufacturer's instructions, fuse to the wrong side of the appropriate fabrics; cut apart on the drawn lines. Position, fuse, and appliqué in place.

Finishing

See Basic Quiltmaking Instructions, pages 65–70, for instructions on binding.

Beginning with a 25″ square of rose batik and marking $2\frac{1}{2}$″-wide strips, make continuous bias binding. Using a bowl or plate, trace and trim a curve at each corner of the throw. Bind with bias-cut rose batik.

Jacobean Elegance

Skill Level 3

Designed by Lisa DeBee Schiller.

Made by Lisa DeBee Schiller and Carol O'Conner.

Machine quilted by Linda Leathersich.

Finished quilt size: $59\frac{1}{4}" \times 63\frac{3}{4}"$

Number of blocks & finished size:
15 Pomegranate blocks $9\frac{1}{4}" \times 9\frac{1}{4}"$

A symbol of abundance, the pomegranate reminds us of all the rewards of the harvest season. There is a lush, bountiful feeling to this lovely lap-sized quilt.

Fabric Requirements and Cutting Instructions

FABRIC	AMOUNT	CUTTING
		See the Pullout at the back of the book for template patterns. Appliqué template patterns are printed without seam allowances.
Assorted light green, cream, and tan prints/plaids (backgrounds)	$1\frac{5}{8}$–$2\frac{1}{8}$ yards total	15 squares $10\frac{3}{4} \times 10\frac{3}{4}$ total
Assorted green prints/textures (appliqué, piecing)	$1\frac{1}{2}$–2 yards total	18 squares $3\frac{1}{2}" \times 3\frac{1}{2}"$ total
		11 Template A, 4 Ar
		11 Template B, 4 Br
		15 Template D
Assorted wine prints/textures (appliqué, piecing)	$\frac{5}{8}$–$\frac{7}{8}$ yard total	17 squares $3\frac{1}{2}" \times 3\frac{1}{2}"$ total
		12 Template C
Assorted turquoise prints/textures (appliqué, piecing)	$\frac{3}{8}$–$\frac{5}{8}$ yard total	14 squares $3\frac{1}{2}" \times 3\frac{1}{2}"$
		15 Template E
Assorted gold prints/textures (appliqué, piecing)	$\frac{1}{4}$–$\frac{3}{8}$ yard total	4 squares $3\frac{1}{2}" \times 3\frac{1}{2}"$
		15 Template F
Brown large floral (piecing, binding)	$1\frac{3}{4}$ yards	*2 strips $4" \times 50"$, cut on lengthwise grain
		30 rectangles $3\frac{1}{2}" \times 6\frac{1}{2}"$
Rose texture (appliqué, piecing)	$\frac{3}{4}$ yard	*6 strips $1\frac{1}{2}" \times 50"$, pieced from 8 width of fabric (WOF) strips
		7 squares $3\frac{1}{2}" \times 3\frac{1}{2}"$
		4 strips $1\frac{1}{8}" \times 6\frac{1}{2}"$
		3 Template C
Brown floral border stripe (border)	**$2\frac{1}{4}$ yards	***4 strips $7" \times 76"$, cut on length-wise grain
Backing (piece horizontally)	$3\frac{7}{8}$ yards	
Batting	Twin size	

OTHER MATERIALS
Brush-tip permanent marking pen, brown
Fine-tip permanent marking pen, brown
Freezer paper (optional)

*Cut first.   ** Yardage based on featured fabric.   ***See Planning.

Lisa's lovely quilt is like a step back into Merrie Olde England. The appliquéd pomegranates are reminiscent of those in the famous unicorn tapestries of the Middle Ages. You'll love playing with Lisa's inking techniques, below, which add depth and delight to the appliqués. Notice that the inked ribbon differs slightly in each block.

PLANNING

Be careful to cut your border strips so that the floral stripe is centered. Our instructions are written so that you will have extra length for your border strips, enabling you to position the borders as you choose at the mitered corners.

Lisa's Inking Technique

Practice these techniques on a piece of scrap muslin before inking on your actual blocks. You may find it easier to draw on your fabric if you first iron a piece of freezer paper to the back of the block to stabilize it. Using a brush-tip permanent marking pen, draw ribbon, alternating the point of the brush with the side to vary the thickness of your ribbon. Always beginning at the top of the stem, draw two or three loops, as desired, to either side, ending with a flourish at each end.

Using a fine-tip permanent marking pen, make tiny dots around appliqué edges, starting with just a few dots.

To create a sense of depth, add more dots around inside curves.

Appliquéing the Blocks

See Basic Quiltmaking Instructions, pages 65–70, for instructions on appliqué.

1. Finger-press assorted $10^3/4$″ squares in half on both the length and width; use the folds as a placement guide. Referring to the illustrations below and photos, position Template A–F fabrics (in alphabetical order). Keep in mind that the square will be trimmed to $9^3/4$″ × $9^3/4$″. Appliqué in place to make pomegranate blocks.

Make 11 total.

Positioning the appliqué

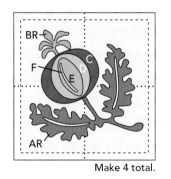

Make 4 total.

Positioning for reverse appliqué

2. **Note:** Lisa used reverse appliqué to expose the gold Template F pomegranate center. Trim the block to $9^3/4$″ × $9^3/4$″, make in the arrangements and quantities shown. Referring to Lisa's Inking Technique, page 55, draw ribbons and dots on the block (see templates for sample placement).

Piecing the Strips

Note: Positioning of the background colors ($3^1/2$″ squares) in strips is random.

1. Draw a diagonal line on the wrong side of a $3^1/2$″ square. Place the marked square on a brown large floral rectangle, right sides together, aligning the raw edges. Stitch on the drawn line; trim away and discard the excess fabric. Press open. Repeat on the opposite end with a $3^1/2$″ square of another color to make flying geese units. Make 30 total.

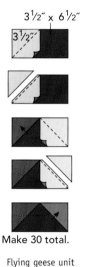

$3^1/2$″ × $6^1/2$″

Make 30 total.

Flying geese unit

2. Stitch a strip of 15 flying geese units. Stitch rose texture $1^1/8$″ × $6^1/2$″ strips to the top and bottom. Make 2 total.

$1^1/8$″ × $6^1/2$″

Make 2 total.

Flying geese strip

Quilt Top Assembly

Refer to the assembly diagram for the following steps.

1. Stitch 3 vertical strips of 5 blocks each, watching the orientation. Sew rose texture $1^1/_2 \times 50''$ strips to the sides of each. Trim even with the top and bottom. Stitch together the block strips and flying geese strips, alternating. Sew brown large floral $4'' \times 50''$ strips to the top/bottom; trim even with the sides.

2. Starting and stopping $^1/_4''$ from the quilt corners, sew brown floral border stripe strips to the sides, top, and bottom of the quilt. Sew and trim miters.

Quilting and Finishing

See Basic Quiltmaking Instructions, pages 65–70, for instructions on quilting and binding.

Layer, baste, and quilt. Linda machine outline quilted the appliqué and added stippling in the background. The flying geese strips feature a continuous curled leaf motif, and a continuous feather design is quilted on the brown floral strips and the center of the border. Linda outline quilted the small leaves in the gold areas of the floral border and quilted continuous waves in the rose strips. Bind with brown large floral.

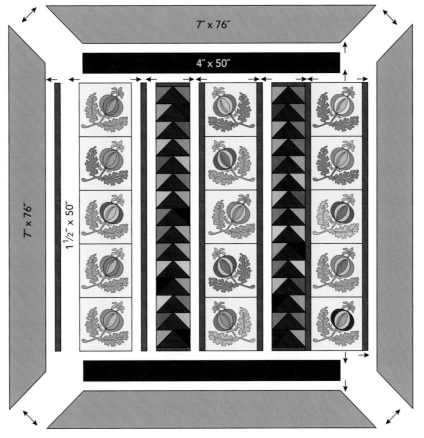

7″ x 76″

4″ x 50″

7″ x 76″

$1^1/_2$″ x 50″

Assembly diagram

Scrap Basket Blooms

Skill Level 2

Designed by Rhonda Dohna.

Machine quilted by Janna Mitchell of Janna's Quilting Co.

Finished quilt size: $52\frac{1}{2}" \times 72\frac{1}{2}"$

Number of blocks & finished size:

36 pieced blocks 8″ × 8″

2 appliquéd blocks 8″ × 48″

Old-fashioned charm never goes out of style. In fact, it's one of the things we love most about quilts. This pieced and appliquéd beauty will tempt you with its clean lines and country details.

Fabric Requirements and Cutting Instructions

Been dreaming about a scrap quilt? Here is the perfect pattern for using all your favorite fabrics together. Rhonda's quilt is a great combination of piecing and appliqué. Divide your fabrics into light, medium, and dark piles. Use lights for the backgrounds and mediums/darks for the pieced blocks and appliqué.

FABRIC	AMOUNT	CUTTING
		See the Pullout at the back of the book for template patterns. Appliqué template patterns are printed without seam allowances.
Dark green texture (piecing)	$\frac{5}{8}$ yard	12 strips $1\frac{1}{2}" \times$ width of fabric (WOF)
Cream texture (piecing)	2 yards	12 strips $1\frac{1}{2}" \times$ WOF
		144 squares $2\frac{1}{2}" \times 2\frac{1}{2}"$
		36 squares $4\frac{7}{8}" \times 4\frac{7}{8}"$
Assorted dark prints (piecing)	$\frac{7}{8}$-$1\frac{1}{4}$ yards total	36 squares $4\frac{7}{8}" \times 4\frac{7}{8}"$ total
Medium brown texture (stems)	$\frac{5}{8}$ yard	1 bias-cut strip $1\frac{1}{2}" \times 186"$
Tan texture (appliqué background)	1 yard	2 strips $9\frac{1}{2}" \times 49\frac{1}{2}"$, pieced from 3 WOF strips
Dark brown print (basket, binding)	$\frac{7}{8}$ yard	2 Template A
Beige/cream texture (hearts)	5″ × 8″ piece	2 Template B
Red/black texture (flowers)	12″ × 13″ piece	8 Template C
Light gold texture (flower centers)	7″ × 7″ piece	8 Template D
Red/cream texture (berries)	8″ × 10″ piece	20 Template D
Gold print (buds)	9″ × 11″ piece	6 each Template F/Fr
Green texture (bud base)	8″ × 10″ piece	6 each Template G/Gr
Medium green print (leaves, sashing, border)	1 yard	4 strips $2\frac{1}{2}" \times 57"$, pieced from 6 WOF strips
		2 strips $2\frac{1}{2}" \times 73"$, pieced from 4 WOF strips
		24 Template E
Backing (piece horizontally)	$3\frac{1}{2}$ yards	
Batting	Twin size	
OTHER MATERIALS		
Bias bar, $\frac{1}{2}"$ (optional)		

Piecing the Blocks

1. Sew dark green and cream 1½″ strips together. Make 12. Press the seams in the direction of the arrow. Cut 288 segments 1½″ wide.

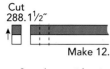

Cut
288. 1½″

Make 12.

Green/cream strip set

2. Stitch 2 segments together to make a four patch.

Make 144.

Four patch

3. Sew 2 four-patch and 2 cream 2½″ squares together to make a pieced square. Make 72.

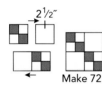

2½″

Make 72.

4. Draw a diagonal line on the wrong side of a cream 4⅞″ square. Place a cream square on an assorted dark 4⅞″ square, right sides together. Sew a ¼″ seam on each side of the marked line; cut apart on the marked line. Press open to make pieced squares. Make 72 squares total.

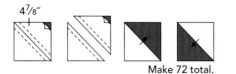

4⅞″

Make 72 total.

Pieced squares

5. Sew 4 pieced squares together to make a pieced block. Make 36 total.

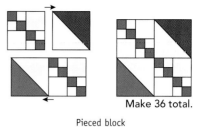

Make 36 total.

Pieced block

6. To make stems, fold a medium brown 1½″ × 186″ bias-cut strip in half, wrong sides together. Stitch ¼″ from the raw edge. Trim the seam allowance to ⅛″. Press the tube flat, centering the seam allowance on the back so the raw edge isn't visible from the front. Using a ½″ bias bar makes pressing faster and easier. Cut 4 sections each of the following lengths: 22¾″, 10½″, 7″, 3¾″, 2½″.

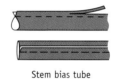

Stem bias tube

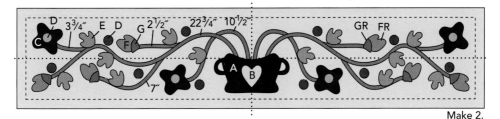

Make 2.

Positioning the appliqué

Appliquéing the Strips

See Basic Quiltmaking Instructions, pages 65–70, for instructions on appliqué.

1. **Note:** The tan appliqué background strips are cut oversized to allow for shrinkage during appliqué. Finger-press tan $9^1/2'' \times 49^1/2''$ strips in half lengthwise and crosswise; use the folds as a placement guide. Position the stems and templates, keeping in mind that the rectangle will be trimmed to $8^1/2'' \times 48^1/2''$ (finished size is $8'' \times 48''$). Appliqué in place. See illustration above.

2. By machine or hand, buttonhole stitch around the appliqué and stems. Trim to $8^1/2'' \times 48^1/2''$. Make 2.

Buttonhole stitch

Quilt Top Assembly

Refer to the assembly diagram for the following steps.

1. Sew 6 rows of 6 pieced blocks each. Sew the rows together. Sew medium green $2^1/2'' \times 57''$ strips to the top and bottom; trim even with the sides. Stitch appliqué blocks to the top and bottom.

2. Sew medium green $2^1/2'' \times 73''$ strips to the sides; trim even with the top and bottom. Stitch the remaining medium green strips to the top/bottom; trim even.

Assembly diagram

Quilting and Finishing

See Basic Quiltmaking Instructions, pages 65–70, for instructions on quilting and binding.

Layer, baste, and quilt. Janna machine quilted a swirling meander on the pieced block backgrounds and four patches. A floral motif was centered on the squares formed by the assorted dark prints. The appliqué blocks were echo quilted, and a vine-and-leaf design fills the green sashing and border. Bind the quilt with dark brown print.

Poinsettia Wreaths

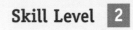

Skill Level 2

Designed by Ann Weber.

Finished quilt size: 46″ × 46″

Number of blocks & finished size:
9 Poinsettia Wreath blocks 12″ × 12″

Welcome guests with these pretty wreaths in seasonal colors. Simple piecing and easy appliqué combine for a quick, appealing holiday project.

Fabric Requirements and Cutting Instructions

Take care to use an exact ¼″ seam allowance when piecing the blocks so the pieced border will fit perfectly.

FABRIC	AMOUNT	CUTTING
		See the Pullout at the back of the book for template patterns. Appliqué template patterns are printed without seam allowances. Piecing template patterns are printed with seam allowances.
Cream mottle (background, pieced border)	1³⁄₈ yards	20 squares 6¼″ × 6¼″
		20 Template D
		4 each Template E/Er
Green print (piecing, leaves)	³⁄₈ yard	10 strips 1″ × 6¼″
		5 strips 1″ × 12½″
		16 Template A
Green texture (piecing, leaves)	³⁄₈ yard	8 strips 1″ × 6¼″
		4 strips 1″ × 12½″
		20 Template A
Tan texture (background)	⁵⁄₈ yard	16 squares 6¼″ × 6¼″
Red/black print (petals)	³⁄₈ yard	72 Template B
Red texture (petals)	³⁄₈ yard	72 Template B
Gold mottle (flower centers)	¹⁄₈ yard	36 Template C
Green stripe (inner border, binding)	³⁄₄ yard	4 strips 1¼″ × width of fabric (WOF)
Red floral print (pieced border, border corners)	⁵⁄₈ yard	4 squares 4½″ × 4½″
		24 Template D
Backing	3 yards	
Batting	Twin size	

Piecing and Appliquéing the Blocks

See Basic Quiltmaking Instructions, pages 65–70, for instructions on appliqué.

1. Sew cream squares and green print strips together to make a pieced background. Make 5. Repeat using tan squares and green texture strips. Make 4.

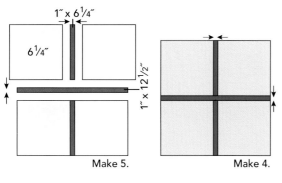

Make 5.   Make 4.

Pieced background

2. Finger-press a cream pieced background square in half diagonally twice; use the folds as a placement guide. Position Templates A–C and appliqué in place. Make 5.

Make 5.

Positioning the appliqué, block 1

3. Repeat Step 2 using tan pieced background squares and template fabrics. Make 4.

Make 4.

Positioning the appliqué, block 2

Quilt Top Assembly

Refer to the assembly diagram for the following steps.

1. Sew 3 rows of 3 blocks each, alternating. Sew the rows together. Stitch green stripe strips to the sides; trim even with the top and bottom. Sew the remaining green strips to the top/bottom; trim even with the sides.

2. To make borders, sew 4 strips using 6 red floral print Template D and 5 cream Template D each. Stitch a cream Template E and ER to the ends. Sew two strips to the sides of the quilt center. Stitch red floral 4½" squares to the ends of the remaining pieced strips and sew to the top/bottom.

Assembly diagram

Quilting and Finishing

See Basic Quiltmaking Instructions, pages 65–70, for instructions on quilting and binding.

Layer, baste, and quilt. Ann machine ditch quilted the appliqué, the green strips in the block piecing, and the borders. The background was filled with a meander. She double outline stitched the "V" shape of the red border triangles with stitching lines ½" apart. Bind the quilt with green stripe.

Basic Quiltmaking Instructions

These instructions offer a brief introduction to quiltmaking. Quiltmaking instructions for projects in this compilation are written for the individual with some sewing experience. Review this information before beginning if you are making your first quilt.

Supplies

- Scissors (for paper and template plastic)
- Iron and ironing board
- Marking tools: pencils, chalk markers, fine-point permanent marker
- Needles: package of sharps (for hand piecing) assorted sizes; package of betweens (for hand quilting), size nos. 8 to 12
- Quilting hoop or frame
- Pins and pincushion
- Rotary cutter and mat (at least 18″ × 24″)
- Rulers: 2″ × 18″; clear acrylic 12″ square; clear acrylic 6″ × 24″ (for use with a rotary cutter)
- Sewing machine (for machine piecing)
- Shears, 8″ (for fabric)
- Template plastic
- Thimble to fit the middle finger of your sewing hand
- Thread: nylon monofilament thread, size .004 (for machine quilting); quilting thread (for hand quilting); sewing thread in colors to match your fabrics

Fabric Preparation

Prewash fabric to remove excess dye and minimize shrinking of the completed project. Machine wash gently in warm water, dry on warm setting, and press. Immerse a swatch of fabric in a clear glass of water to test colorfastness; if dye appears, soak fabric in equal parts of white vinegar and water. Rinse and dry fabric; test another swatch. If dye still appears, do not use the fabric.

Pressing

Proper pressing is a prerequisite for accurate piecing. Press with a light touch, using iron tip and an up-and-down movement. Use either steam or dry heat, whichever works best, and assembly-type pressing to save time.

Choose a pressing plan before beginning a project and stay consistent, if possible. Seams are "set" by first being pressed flat and then pressed either to one side, usually toward the darker fabric, or open. Sometimes, both are used in the same project, depending on the design.

To prevent distortion, press long, sewn strips widthwise and avoid raw bias edges. Other pressing hints: Use distilled water; avoid a too-hot iron, which will cause fabric shininess; and pretreat wrinkled or limp fabric with a liberal amount of spray fabric sizing.

Templates

Make templates by placing transparent plastic over the printed template pattern and tracing with a fine-point permanent marker. Trace and cut out on the stitching line (broken line) for hand-piecing templates; cut on the outer solid line for machine-piecing templates.

Label each template with the name of the quilt, template letter, grain line, and match points (dots) where sewing lines intersect. Pierce a small hole at each match point for marking match points on fabric.

Fabric Marking and Cutting

Position fabric wrong side up and place the template on the fabric. With a marker or well-sharpened pencil, trace around the template and mark match points. For hand-piecing templates, allow enough space for $1/4''$ seam allowances to be added. For machine-piecing templates, cut along the drawn line. For hand-piecing, cut $1/4''$ beyond the drawn line.

Piecing

Stitch fabric pieces together for patchwork by hand or machine.

HAND PIECING

Place two fabric pieces right sides together. With the point of a pin, match corner or other match points to align seamlines; pin. Use about an 18″-long single strand of quality sewing thread and sewing needle of your choice. To secure thread, begin at a match point and, without a knot, take a stitch and a backstitch on the seamline. Make smooth running stitches, closely and evenly spaced, stitching on the drawn line on both patches of fabric. Backstitch at the end of the seamline. Do not stitch into the seam allowances. Press seams after the block is completed.

To join seamed pieces and strengthen the intersection, stitch through the seam allowances and backstitch directly before and immediately after them.

MACHINE PIECING

Use a $1/4''$-wide presser foot for a seaming guide, or place a strip of opaque tape on the machine throatplate $1/4''$ from the needle position. Place two fabric pieces right sides together, raw edges aligned, and pin perpendicular to the future seamline to secure. Begin and end stitching at the raw edges without backstitching; do not sew over pins. Make sure the thread tension and stitches are smooth and even on both sides of the seam. When joining seamed pieces, butt or match seams, pin to secure, and stitch. Press each seam before continuing to the next.

To chain piece, repeatedly feed pairs of fabric pieces under the presser foot while taking a few stitches without any fabric under the needle between pairs. Cut the chained pieces apart before or after pressing.

Appliquéing
HAND APPLIQUÉ

Needle-Turn Method. Place the template on the fabric's right side. Draw around the template with a non-permanent marking tool of your choice, making a line no darker than necessary to be visible. Cut out the shape, including a scant $1/4''$ seam allowance on all sides. Experience makes "eyeballing" the seam allowance quick and easy.

To blind stitch the appliqué shapes, position the appliqué shape on the background fabric, securing with a pin or a dab of glue stick. Select a sewing thread color to match the appliqué fabric. A 100% cotton thread is less visible than a cotton/polyester blend.

Begin stitching on a straight or gently curved edge, not at a sharp point or corner. Turn under a short length of seam allowance using your fingers and the point of your needle. Insert the needle into the seamline of the appliqué piece, coming up from the wrong side and catching just one or two threads on the edge. Push the needle through the background fabric exactly opposite the point where the thread was stitched onto the appliqué fabric piece. Coming up from the wrong side, take a stitch through the background fabric and appliqué piece, again catching just a couple threads of the appliqué fabric. Allow about $1/8''$ between stitches. The thread is visible on the wrong side of your block and almost invisible on the right side.

As you stitch around the edge of an appliqué fabric piece, turn under the seam allowance as you work, following the drawn line on the right side of the fabric, using your fingers and the point of the needle.

Freezer Paper Method I. Trace the template shape onto the dull side of freezer paper and cut out. With a dry iron, press the freezer paper shape, shiny side down, onto the appliqué fabric's right side. Cut out the fabric, including a scant ¼″ seam allowance on all sides. To stitch, follow the same procedure used in the needle-turn method. Rather than using the drawn line as your guide, use the edge of the freezer paper.

Freezer Paper Method II. Trace the reversed template shape onto the dull side of freezer paper and cut out. With a dry iron, press the freezer paper shape, shiny side down, onto the appliqué fabric's wrong side. Cut out the fabric, including a scant ¼″ seam allowance on all sides. Finger-press the seam allowance to the back of the paper template and baste in place. To stitch an appliqué fabric piece, follow the same procedure used in the needle-turn method. The seam allowance has already been turned under in this technique. To remove the freezer paper, remove the basting shortly before closing the appliqué, and pluck out the freezer paper with a tweezers. Or after the appliqué is sewn, cut the background fabric away behind the appliqué and remove the paper.

To *reverse appliqué,* two fabric pieces are layered on the background fabric, and the edges of the top fabric are cut in a particular design and turned under to reveal the underlying fabric. Pin or glue the bottom appliqué fabric into position on the background block. Cut the top fabric along the specified cutting lines. Place the top fabric over the bottom fabric; check the position of the bottom fabric by holding the block up to a light source and pin. Use the needle-turn method to turn under the top fabric seam allowance and appliqué.

MACHINE APPLIQUÉ

Trace reversed templates without seam allowances on the paper side of paper-backed fusible web. Cut out, leaving a small margin beyond the drawn lines. Following the manufacturer's instructions, apply to the wrong side of the appliqué fabric. Cut out on the drawn line. Position appliqué on the quilt where desired, and fuse to the quilt following the manufacturer's instructions. Finish the appliqué edges by machine using a buttonhole stitch, satin stitch, or stitch of your choice.

How to Make Continuous Bias

1. Measure the quilt to determine how many inches of bias you need. If using as binding, allow 10″ extra for turning corners and the closure. Refer to the chart below to find the size square needed.
2. Cut the square in half diagonally (A). With right sides together, sew the triangles together with a ¼″ seam (B) and press open (C).

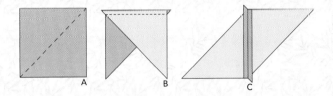

3. On the fabric's wrong side long edges, draw lines to make strips of your chosen binding width (D). Use a clear acrylic rotary ruler and a pencil or fine-point permanent pen to draw the lines.

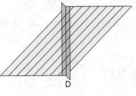

4. Bring the short diagonal edges together, forming a tube. Offset the drawn lines by one strip (E). With right sides together, match lines with pins at the ¼″ seamline and stitch the seam; press open (F).

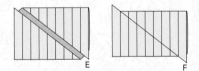

5. With scissors, cut along the continuously drawn line (G).

SIZE SQUARE TO CUT

Bias Strip Width	80″ Length Needed	260″ Length Needed	275″ Length Needed	320″ Length Needed
1″	9″ square			
1¼″		19″ square	19″ square	20″ square
1½″		20″ square	21″ square	22″ square
1¾″		22″ square	22″ square	24″ square
2½″		26″ square	27″ square	30″ square
3″		28″ square	28″ square	34″ square

Mitering Corners

Miter border corners when an angled seam complements the overall design of the quilt. Cut border strips the finished length and width of the quilt plus twice the border width and 4″–6″ extra.

Center and pin border strips in place. Start and end seams $\frac{1}{4}″$ from raw edges; backstitch to secure. Press the seams toward the quilt top. Lay the quilt top right side up on an ironing board and fold each border end flat back onto itself, right sides together, forming a 45° angle at the quilt's corner. Press to form sharp creases. Fold the quilt on the diagonal, right sides together. Align border strip raw edges, border seams at the $\frac{1}{4}″$ backstitched point, and creases; pin in place. Stitch along crease, backstitching at $\frac{1}{4}″$ border seam. Press the seam open. With the quilt right side up, align the 45°-angle line of the square ruler on the seamline to check accuracy. If the corner is flat and square, trim excess fabric to $\frac{1}{4}″$ seam allowance.

For multiple mitered borders, sew strips together first and attach to the quilt as one unit.

Marking Quilting Patterns

Press the quilt top and change any correctable irregularities. Choose a marking tool that makes a thin accurate line and pretest removability on quilt fabric scraps.

Marking tool options include water-soluble and air-erasable markers, white dressmaker's pencil, chalk pencils, chalk rolling markers, and slivers of hardened soap. Try silver and yellow Berol pencils on dark fabrics and a No. 2 pencil sparingly on light fabric. The same project may need several types of markers.

Design aid options include freezer-paper cutouts, stencils, templates, household items such as cookie cutters, and acrylic rulers.

After marking quilting designs of choice, do not press the quilt top, as markings could be set permanently.

Backing

Use the same quality backing fabric as used in the quilt top. Remove selvages and cut the backing at least 4″ larger than the quilt top on all sides. It is necessary to seam backing for quilts larger than 36″ wide when using standard 40″–42″-wide fabric. Use either vertical or horizontal seaming, whichever requires less fabric. Press backing seams open.

Batting

Standard precut batting sizes are:

Crib	45″ × 60″
Twin	72″ × 90″
Full/Double	81″ × 96″
Queen	90″ × 108″
King	120″ × 120″

Consider several factors when choosing batting. How do you want the quilt to look? How close will the quilting stitches be? Are you hand or machine quilting? How will the quilt be used?

Batting is made from different fibers (not all fibers are available in all sizes). If you prefer an old-fashioned-looking quilt, consider using a mostly cotton batting. The newer cotton battings are bonded and do not require the close quilting that old-fashioned cotton battings once did. If you don't want to do a lot of quilting, use a regular or low-loft polyester batting. If you like "puffy" quilts, use a high-loft polyester batting. Wool battings are also available.

If you are not sure which batting is right for your project, consult the professionals at your local quilt shop.

Layering the Quilt Sandwich

Mark the center of the backing on the wrong side at the top, bottom, and side edges. On a smooth, flat surface a little larger than the quilt, place backing right side down. Smooth any wrinkles until the backing is flat; use masking tape to hold it taut and in place.

Unfold batting and lay over backing. Smooth wrinkles, keeping the backing wrinkle free.

Position the quilt top on the backing and batting, keeping all layers wrinkle free. Match centers of the quilt top with the backing. Use straight pins to keep layers from shifting while basting.

Basting

Basting holds the three layers together to prevent shifting while quilting.

For *hand quilting,* baste using a long needle threaded with as long a length of sewing thread as can be used without tangling. Insert the needle through all layers in the center of the quilt and baste layers together with a long running stitch. For the first line of basting, stitch up and down the vertical center of the quilt. Next, baste across the horizontal center of the quilt. Working toward the edges and creating a grid, continue basting to completely stabilize the layers.

For *machine quilting*, pin-baste using nickel-plated safety pins, instead of needle and thread. Begin in the center of the quilt, and work outward to the edges, placing safety pins approximately every 4″.

Quilting

HAND QUILTING

Hand quilting features evenly spaced, small stitches on both sides of the quilt, with no knots showing on the backside.

Most quilters favor 100% cotton thread in ecru or white, though beautiful colors are available.

Beginners start with a size 8 or 9 "between" needle and advance to a shorter, finer size 10 or 12 needle for finer stitching. Use a well-fitting, puncture-proof thimble on the middle finger of your sewing hand to position and push the needle through the quilt layers.

A frame or hoop keeps the layered quilt smooth and taut; choose from a variety of shapes and sizes. Select a comfortable seat with proper back support and a good light source, preferably natural light, to reduce eye strain.

To begin, cut thread 24″ long and make a knot on one end. Place the needle tip either into a seamline or ½″

behind the point where quilting stitches are to begin. Guide it through the batting and up through the quilt top to "bury" the knot. Gently pull on the thread until you hear the knot "pop" through the quilt top. Trim the thread tail.

To quilt using a running stitch, hold the needle parallel to the quilt top and stitch up and down through the three layers with a rocking motion, making several stitches at a time. This technique is called "stacking." Gently and smoothly pull the thread through the layers. To end, make a small knot and bury it in the batting.

MACHINE QUILTING

Machine quilting requires an even-feed or walking foot to ensure quilting a straight stitch without distorting the layers, and a darning foot for free-motion or heavily curved stitching.

Use 100% cotton thread or size .004 nylon monofilament thread (clear for light-colored fabrics, smoky for dark fabrics) on the top and cotton in the bobbin. Pretest stitch length and thread tension using two muslin pieces layered with batting. Adjust as needed.

Choose a quilting strategy. Begin stitching in the middle and work outward, making sure the layers are taut. Roll the edges of the quilt compactly to reveal the area being quilted; reroll as needed. To secure the thread, take

one or two regular-length stitches forward and backward, and continue forward; stitch a few very small stitches and gradually increase to desired length. Trim thread tails.

Stitch "in the ditch" or along the seamline to secure quilt layers while adding subtle texture. Stitch open areas with a design of your choice.

Making Binding Strips

Quilt binding can be cut on the bias or straight of grain. Use a continuous strip of bias for a quilt that will be used frequently or has scalloped edges and rounded corners. Refer to How To Make Continuous Bias, page 68, for making continuous bias binding. For bias or straight-grain double-fold binding, cut $2\frac{1}{2}$"- or 3"-wide strips of fabric and fold in half, wrong sides together.

Attaching the Binding

Beginning near the middle of any side, align binding and quilt raw edges. Sew to the corner and stop stitching $\frac{1}{4}$" from the quilt edge; backstitch to secure (an even-feed foot is very helpful). Remove from the sewing machine. Fold the binding strip up and back down over itself, aligning raw edges on the second side, and pin in place. Beginning $\frac{1}{4}$" from the quilt edge (same point where stitching stopped on the first side), sew binding to the second side and stop stitching $\frac{1}{4}$" from the next corner edge; backstitch. Remove from the sewing machine and continue in the same manner. After sewing all sides, finish using the technique of your choice. Wrap binding around to the back side, using your fingers to manipulate each corner to achieve a miter on both front and back sides. Pin and blind stitch in place.

Signing Your Quilt

You will want to sign and date your quilt and record other information important to you, such as the quilt's name, your city and state, and the event the quilt commemorates. You may embroider or use permanent ink to record this information on a piece of fabric that you then stitch to the quilt backing; or you may embroider directly on the quilt.

Resources

For a list of other fine books from C&T Publishing,
ask for a free catalog:
C&T Publishing, Inc.
P.O. Box 1456
Lafayette, CA 94549
(800) 284-1114
Email: ctinfo@ctpub.com
Website: www.ctpub.com
C&T Publishing's professional photography services
are now available to the public.
Visit us at www.ctmediaservices.com.

For quilting supplies:
Cotton Patch
1025 Brown Avenue
Lafayette, CA 94549
(800) 835-4418 or
(925) 283-7883
Email: CottonPa@aol.com
Website: www.quiltusa.com
Note: Fabrics used in the quilts shown may not
be currently available, as fabric manufacturers keep
most fabrics in print for only a short time.

To contact or subscribe to McCall's Quilting:
McCall's Quilting
741 Corporate Circle, Suite A
Golden, CO 80401
(800) 944-0736
Email: mcq@ckmedia.com
Website: www.mccallsquilting.com
McCall's Quilting is published bi-monthly by CK Media.

Great Titles
from
C&T PUBLISHING

At Play with Appliqué
Dilys A. Fronks
7 Template-Free Techniques ▪ 10 Step-by-Step Projects
Hand & Machine Methods

Quilts with a Spin
7 New Projects from Piece O' Cake Designs
LJJ 2004
BECKY GOLDSMITH & LINDA JENKINS

Carol Burniston
Color-Splashed QUILTS
FUSE FUN APPLIQUÉ TO YOUR PIECING

KIM SCHAEFER
Flowering Quilts
16 FRESH FOLK ART PROJECTS TO DECORATE YOUR H...

Kathy K. Wylie
Sewflakes
PAPERCUT-APPLIQUÉ QUILTS

Carol Armstrong's
Patches & Posies
DESIGNS FOR APPLIQUÉ & QUILTING